THREE LIVES LEFT ?

THREE LIVES LEFT?

SIX TIMES, BY THE GRACE OF GOD,
I SURVIVED LIFE THREATENING SITUATIONS!
DO I NOW HAVE, THREE LIVES LEFT?

THOMAS R THURMAN

Published by:
Warren Springs Publishing
4398 County Road 237
Monroe City, Missouri 63456
Toll free: (855) 228-7167

Copyright © 2012 by Thomas R Thurman
All rights reserved. No portion of this book may be reproduced in any form without the written permission of the publisher, except by a reviewer who may quote brief passages in a review.

ISBN: 978-0-9858128-0-5

Cover Art by:
Michael Meyer
meyersart.com

Printed in the USA by Walsworth Publishing Company
Marceline, Missouri 64658

Contents

Dedication ix

Acknowledgments xi

Introduction xii

MAP OF WHERE I GREW UP xv

1   Early Memories 1

2   Neighbors Sharing the Work 11

3   The Old Country School 17

4   To Grandma and Grandpa's House 27

5   A Crop of My Own 31

6   The Town of Warren 35

7   My Sister Beth 43

8   Skunks 51

9   The Buzzards Nest 57

10   Discoveries in the Wild 65

11   The Car Hood Boat 73

12   Dogs 79

13   To Run Like the Wind 87

14	Those Crazy Teens	95
15	The Timely Breakdown	107
16	The Lure of the Canyon	111
17	Rescue in the Grand Canyon	121
18	Our Changing World	137
19	Reflections	147
20	Poems by Lillian E (Thurman) Johnson	153
	Questing	154
	Parting	155
21	Poems by Thomas R Thurman	157
	Death Came Knocking	158
	Your Friend	159
	The Trails in Our Lives	160
	Footprints in the Sand	161
	He Sent the Robins	162
	The Little Butterfly	163
	Those Eyes	164
	I'll Love You More	165
	Unspoken Words	166
About the Author		167

Dedicated To

My wife, Connie L Thurman,

The most unselfish person I have ever known

Acknowledgments

A special thanks to everyone who helped me in any way with this book:

- To my son, Brad, and my daughter, Cindi, for suggesting I write down some memories from the past. This was my motivation for beginning this book.

- To my sister, Beth, for spending many hours editing the manuscript. I couldn't have done it without her!

- To my brother-in-law, Mike, for the cover artwork, and for formatting the manuscript for printing.

- To my daughter-in-law, Jacki, for designing the map of the area where I grew up and for creating the logo for Warren Springs Publishing Company.

- To my son-in-law, Paul, for his technical advice when I had computer problems.

- To Consetta Gottman Creations for the photos on pages 40, 102 and 104.

- And to my wife, Connie, for her suggestions, and for putting up with me while I spent many hours preparing the manuscript for this book.

Introduction

When I started to write this book, my intention was to just tell the story of my life. Then, as it started to come together, I realized how fortunate I was to have survived all the life threatening situations I had experienced. God must have a plan for my life, as it's the only explanation for why He would make sure I got through each one of them alive. As you read about each experience, you will see that my only chance of survival was by the grace of God.

At times, I may seem proud and boastful about the things I have done in my life. For this I ask for forgiveness from God, for without Him, none of those things would have been possible. So to God be all the glory!

I sometimes wonder if I'm doing what God wants me to, as I don't seem to be doing anything of significant importance. Hopefully, He is guiding me to tell my story in a way that will be of some benefit to all those who read it.

I was born on a farm in rural Missouri in 1942. This was at a time when the old ways and the new in rural America were just beginning to come together. This book tells about the way of life, at that time, on the farm and in the schools. It is also about how things were so much different when we were growing up during those times than they are now. Some parts of this book will make you laugh, and some parts may make you cry.

Within the pages of this book there is something for everyone. It includes stories of adventure, stories about nature, stories of forgotten things from the past, and some of the most unusual and amusing things you'll ever read. I also included two lost poems I discovered that were written by my aunt, who is now deceased, along with a few of the poems I have written.

So, I have done my best to present this factual story in a way that will be interesting to all types of readers of all ages. It is my hope that as you read these stories, they will make a difference in your life, just as they have in mine while living them and writing about them.

The farm where I grew up. Photo taken in 1950.

MAP OF WHERE I GREW UP

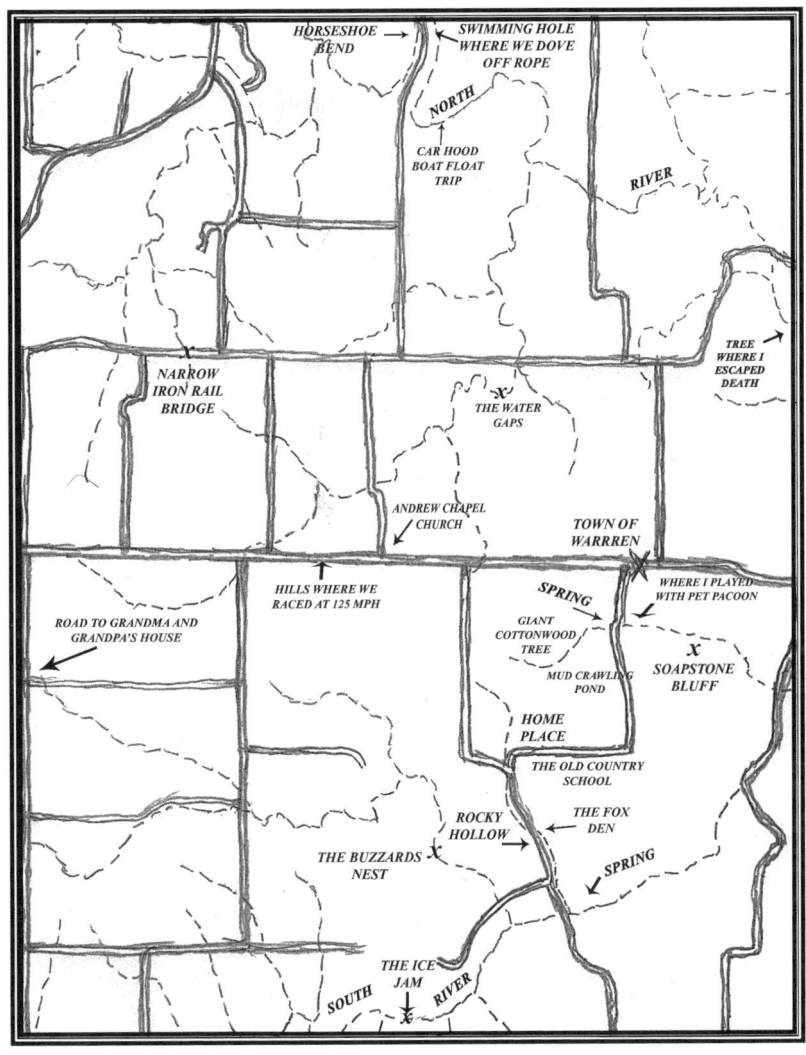

Chapter

1

Early Memories

"Where's Tommy?" Mom screamed, as she ran to where Dad was cutting the oats with the binder. I haven't seen him, Dad exclaimed! I thought he was at the house with you.

I had wandered away from the yard where I was playing and gone looking for Dad. I was only three years old at the time, so they were obviously upset when they couldn't find me. Mom had searched everywhere around the house, the lots, and even in the hayloft of the barn which I had recently learned to climb into. As they searched for me, they were in a near panic as they thought of all the things that could have happened to me. They said when they finally found me I was out in the oat field where the oats were taller than I was, just walking around trying to find Dad. They said they were pretty upset

My parents, Winifred and Ralph Thurman in 1934.

with me, but I didn't seem too concerned. The whole thing happened so long ago, its hard for me to tell which parts I really remember from the parts I was told.

Chapter 1 - EARLY MEMORIES

When I think back to my very earliest memories on the farm, these are the things that come to mind. We had no electricity and no running water, so obviously we did without many of the things everyone takes for granted today. Just imagine not having hot and cold running water, no inside bathroom and no air conditioning, not to mention no TV or even an electric radio. We also had no refrigerator and no freezer. We did have an ice-box where we could keep our food cold for a few days during the summer. I can still remember the "ice-man" who delivered our ice once a week during the summer. To my small eyes, the blocks of ice he delivered for our ice-box were huge. During the winter, keeping our food cold was no problem. We just put it out in the unheated north porch.

Mom had to do all of her cooking and baking on a wood cook stove, even during the hottest days during the summer. Our only source of heat during the winter was from that old wood cook stove and two other wood heating stoves.

We had to pump our water from a cistern in the back yard. Something as simple as taking a bath required heating water on a wood stove in both winter and summer. The water was then poured into a large bathtub, where if you were lucky, you got to take the first bath. After everyone had their baths, the water had to be carried outside where it was poured through the fence. It was so much trouble that unless you were really dirty, you only got to take a bath on Saturday night. In the summer, we would sometimes take daily bathes in our ponds or in the river. Our only lighting was from the coal oil lamps we kept in the house and the coal oil lanterns we used to do our chores outside.

I remember having to go out behind the chicken house to our outhouse when you had to go to the bathroom. I dreaded to cross the chicken yard, as we had one rooster that thought he was the boss of the chicken yard. When I was very small, if he could catch me, he'd give me a good flogging just because he could. (When I got bigger I got even with that ornery old rascal.) The outhouse had cracks between the boards wide enough to see through in case someone else approached while you were there. Very few modern restrooms today have that convenience.

In addition to the chickens, we had geese, turkeys, ducks, guineas, cattle, hogs, sheep, horses and mules. Almost all of the crops that were raised on the farm

Chapter 1 - EARLY MEMORIES

Old Binder used to cut and tie oats into bundles.

were fed to them. We raised mostly corn, oats and hay at that time.

Our oats were seeded in early spring. When they were ready for threshing, they were cut with a binder that tied them into bundles. I can barely remember helping restack the bundles into shocks after a storm. I can also barely remember the threshing machine and the large crew of men that came on that day to thresh our oats. I remember myself and a friend of mine getting into trouble when we climbed into a large pile of oat straw blown there by the threshing machine. The men scolded us saying we could have gotten buried and smothered in the stack of straw that the threshing machine was blowing out. The oats were fed to the livestock and the straw was used for bedding.

I can't remember the corn planter Dad used when he planted with horses, but I can remember when I was very small helping Dad shuck corn by hand. Dad had a pair of mules that pulled the wagon through the field as we shucked the corn. They would pull the wagon forward, without a command from Dad, keeping the wagon positioned just right for us to throw each ear into it. I would shuck the row next to the wagon and Dad would shuck three rows as we slowly went across the field. I was between Dad and the wagon, but I can't ever remember him hitting me with an ear of corn. He was so good at it that he didn't even have to look at the wagon. It seemed like it was always muddy at corn picking time. My boots would get so heavy with mud I could hardly walk.

The corn was mostly fed to the hogs and cattle, with smaller amounts being fed to the other livestock and the poultry. We usually shucked some of it early before it dried down, and chopped it up an ear at a time for the calves we weaned each fall. Most of the corn that was fed to the hogs was just thrown out in the ear. They would chew it off the cob not

Chapter 1 - EARLY MEMORIES

wasting a grain even in the mud. We had to grind the corn fed to the cattle, cob and all. Scooping corn into a bur mill in those early years was done weekly. When I started to school, Dad would have a wagon load of ear corn for me to scoop into a corn crib when I got home at night.

Mom and I used to pick wild blackberries during the summer when I was small. We picked them in three gallon milk buckets. During the best pickings we would get two to four buckets full in one day. We were always hot and miserable after a few hours picking them, and we usually got at least one bee sting each time we went. Boy, was that blackberry jelly and jam she made good though! She also made us blackberry cobblers. When we got to make homemade ice cream to put on our blackberry cobblers, well it was the about the best thing I had ever tasted!

Dad and I both liked to fish in South River for catfish. Sometimes we would set out bank lines just before dark. We would then fish for awhile before going home for the night. The next morning we would be back to check to see how many catfish we had caught by the time the sun was just coming up. Sometimes we would only have a few, but on a good night, we would catch more than we could eat in several meals.

I remember one fishing trip we took really well. Dad told me to get a jar or something to put bait in. I went to the shed to get a jar and when I picked it up, a bumble bee stung me right over my eye. My eye almost swelled shut and Dad said we could go another time. I wasn't going to let any old bumble bee spoil my fishing trip and said I wanted to go anyway. I can't remember if we caught any fish that night or not, but I can still remember the pain.

Dad and I also hunted together some, but he didn't like to hunt as much as he liked to fish. The hunt we took together that I remember most was one fall when we went squirrel hunting. Dad had an old single barrel twelve gauge full choke shotgun, and I had the first shotgun I had ever owned. It was a twenty gauge bolt action J. C. Higgins as near as I can remember. We were back on the fifty acres on the north side of our home place, hunting along a big creek that crossed our farm. The tallest tree on that creek was a giant cottonwood. As we approached it, we saw it was full of squirrels. To my young eyes, it appeared as tall as the giant Redwood trees I had

Chapter 1 - EARLY MEMORIES

read about in California. Dad let me shoot first and it was soon apparent I had hit one, but it was so high that my twenty gauge would not bring him down. After I tried several more unsuccessful shots, we decided my shotgun just didn't have enough power to kill one at that height. Dad shot one with his full choke twelve gauge, and it had just enough more power and range to get one. I think he shot five or six out of that one tree that day. I'm sure he didn't get all of the squirrels, that were in that tree as several that we had seen got into the hollow areas high in the limbs.

    I lost confidence in my twenty gauge shotgun after that experience and started hunting squirrels with Dads old crack shot twenty-two rifle. I got good enough with it that I could hit almost every squirrel I shot in the head no matter how tall the tree was. Several years later, I bought my own twenty-two rifle, a model sixty one Winchester. I shot thousands of rounds through those two rifles until I became so confident that I was sure that I was going to hit anything I shot at with a rifle. I later got to where I was a fairly good shot with a shotgun, but I never did reach the level I had achieved with a rifle.

Chapter 2

Neighbors Sharing the Work

Our only source of heat on the farm was from wood stoves, so wood cutting was a big job each fall. When I got big enough, Dad said I could help him cut down some trees with the two man crosscut saw. The one we had was six or seven feet long with a handle on each end. When one person pulled, the other one was supposed to push. At first it was hard for me to get on to doing it, and Dad said I was "riding the saw." It was amazing how many trees you could cut down and cut into long poles and logs with a crosscut saw and an ax. The poles and logs had to be small enough for two men to be able to handle them.

When everyone in the neighborhood got their pile of logs cut for the winter, the neighbors would get together for wood cutting. The logs were cut into sticks of wood with a buzz saw. The saw had a large circular blade that was driven by a tractor, which was powered by a wide belt. Before the age of the power takeoff, belt drives were used to power equipment such as burr mills, corn shellers, and buzz saws. Two men would feed the logs into the saw, and one would throw the sticks of wood aside to one or two men who would load it on a wagon. The larger sticks of wood had to be split with an ax or wedges before they would go into the stoves. All during the winter, Beth and I had to carry wood from the woodpile to the house for the cook stove and the heating stoves.

Haying was a huge job when I was young, and the neighbors always helped each other at haying time. Before I was old enough to help, most of the hay was put up loose in barns or in hay stacks. It was raked into windrows with a sulky rake, where the men picked it up with pitchforks and threw it onto a wagon. From there it was either taken to a barn or to the place where they were making a haystack. The hay that was put into the barn was fed in mangers inside the barn to the horses, mules, and sheep. The hay that was put into the stacks was hauled in during the winter on a wagon or a large horse drawn sled, where it was fed to the cattle in large wooden hay feeders.

By the time I was old enough to help with the haying, everyone had switched to small bales. Our hay was baled using either small round or small square bales. They usually weighed around seventy five pounds each. We hauled in all our bales each year and so did everyone in our neighborhood. So I got in on hauling (it was called bucking bales) around fifteen thousand bales each year from the mid 1950's until the late 1960's. After that time, we started using large round bales, and the hay crews became a thing of the past.

Each year, all the neighbors would get together on each farm during the fall to butcher hogs and cattle. I can't remember how they were able to preserve all the meat before we had an electric freezer. I suppose that's why they butchered when it was beginning to get cold. I know they cured the hams, but I'm not sure about the rest of the meat.

When they butchered the hogs, they would cut the fat into pieces about two inches square. The pieces were put into a lard kettle (a large black iron container) where a wood fire was kept burning for several hours to cook down the pieces of fat. Someone had to stir the pieces occasionally while they were cooking down to keep them from sticking or burning. Eventually, the fat became cracklings as the liquid lard cooked out. When all the liquid had cooked out, they were less than an inch square. They were slightly brown, and if you took them up while they were hot, they weren't greasy.

I remember standing out by the fire that was under that kettle while the pieces of fat cooked down. It was a cold, snowy day in the middle of winter, and the warmth of the fire felt good as I waited in anticipation to eat some of the cracklings. One of the men took the paddle he was using to stir them and lifted some of those crispy treats out of the hot liquid for me to eat. As soon as the cold winter air had cooled them enough that they wouldn't burn my mouth, I would devour as many as I could.

When all the liquid had cooked out, of the cracklings, they were dipped out. Then the liquid lard was put into large five gallon crocks to cool. When the liquid cooled, it solidified and turned white. The lard was used for cooking and baking throughout the year.

The cured hams were hung from the rafters in the smokehouse. When my parents took one down to cut off some meat, I would eat the raw cured meat. Now, they say you shouldn't eat raw pork, but I just didn't know any better at the time. Maybe all the salt they used to cure the hams made it safe to eat. I guess there's no point in getting concerned about that after all this time has passed, since I'm still here to tell this story!

Chapter 3

The Old Country School

I attended Kincaid school located in Marion County Missouri two miles south of Warren in all but two years from 1948 through 1956. It was closed temporarily in 1950 and 1951 and permanently in 1956.

Old Kincaid School House as it is today.

The old country school sits on a hill deserted and alone, surrounded by elm sprouts and weeds. Its shingles have been worn away by the passing of time no longer protecting its interior from the storms. Its windows are shattered and its paint has peeled away.

As I enter to look around, I notice the door has fallen away. The winds blow across the room creating strange sounds as it passes. As I stand there remembering how it was in my school years, it's as if the winds are now the voices of the past. Memories come flooding back and I realize I must record how it was back then for soon this era of time will be lost to those who come in future generations.

It's early January 1948 and my desk is by the window. The winds are blowing great drifts across the land. The old coal stove now burns so hot it becomes bright red in order protect us from the frigid, sub zero temperature. My thoughts are of how long it is till spring when school will be out and I can be free of this place. At the time I didn't particularly like school. Yes, there were the good times, but my thoughts were usually of some adventure I was planning in the far north forest of Canada and Alaska. Suddenly, reality

Chapter 3 - THE OLD COUNTRY SCHOOL

Me with 1st Grade Teacher

struck and I realized our class was next and I needed to study.

The school was one room with one teacher and eight grades. The coal stove sat in the back on a concrete floor. The rest of the school had a wood floor with a raised area in the front where the teacher's desk was beside a full width blackboard. The raised area in the front was also used as a stage for plays and other performances given at different times during the year. There were only three of us in my first grade class, and as near as I can remember around twelve in the whole school. We basically studied the three R's reading; righting; and rithmetic. (slang for writing and arithmetic)

Discipline seemed to be a problem for our teacher at that time. One student in particular caused numerous problems. Some were quite serious and some, looking back, were rather hilarious. This student and the teacher on one occasion ended up in a fight. The teacher tried to put him in a gunny sack (a large burlap bag.) That turned out to be a bad idea as she ended up being the one in the sack. Another time, the same student decided that since the teacher always ended our recess by ringing the school bell he would make it so she couldn't ring it. When no one was looking, he took the bell from the teachers desk and threw it down in the hole in the boys outhouse. When it was time for recess to be over, the teacher searched everywhere for the bell. In some manner she was able to determine what had happened. She then made her very bad pupil reach down into the "you know what" and fish the bell out. I can't remember if there was any additional punishment or not. She might have thought that that unpleasant task was punishment enough.

    Another time one of the older boys threw a box of 22 caliber rifle shells in the stove. This caused a scary situation while they were exploding in the fire. He only got a scolding for doing this. My how times have changed.

Chapter 3 - THE OLD COUNTRY SCHOOL

It's funny how most of my memories of those two years mostly don't involve class work, as you can see. The only thing that I remember doing that I should have gotten in trouble for was when two of us were sent out to find a suitable Christmas tree. We managed to take up the entire day finding just the right tree. It was much more fun walking in the woods all day than being in school.

We had to bring our lunches to school in paper bags or lunch boxes if our parents could afford them. Seems strange that some of those lunch boxes are worth a lot of money now. I'm sure they didn't cost even a dollar back then.

We played several games during recess and noon including ; annie over ; red rover ; dodge ball and rode our bikes up the jump ramps we made. The boys made a wood fort on the back of the coal shed where no girls were allowed. "Cowboys and Indians" was a game we seemed to never get tired of playing. We took our toy guns to school back then and no one thought anything about it even though some of them looked like the real thing.

During the summer between my second and third grade the school board decided there wasn't enough students to keep Kincaid school open. I had to ride the bus to Monroe City for my third and fourth grades. I didn't like going to the larger school. It was devastating to see how far behind we were in what we had studied. I had always gotten the best grades in our class in the country school. Now I was humiliated to find myself in the slower side of the class because we just hadn't studied much of what had been taught in the larger school in town. It took me most of the third grade to catch up. During my fourth grade, two families moved into the Kincaid school district. It was decided to reopen Kincaid for the next school year.

So I was back in the country school again for the fifth through the eighth grades. Mrs. Darlene was my teacher during my fifth and sixth grades. She stayed in the Scrace house, near the school, during those two years. She was a much better teacher than we had when I was in the first and second grades. We were actually learning something. Her son Dicky stayed with her and attended school at Kincaid during both of those years. We quickly became best friends during those years. Some of my fondest memories are of some the crazy things we did.

Chapter 3 - THE OLD COUNTRY SCHOOL

We both loved to swim and spent as much time swimming in the ponds and rivers as we could. At first our parents would only allow us to swim with an adult along if the water was over our heads. We decided to get around this by going to an old pond that was mostly filled in with mud because hogs and cattle had been wallowing in it. The mud was four or five feet deep with a foot of water on top. We decided that this was shallow enough that our parents couldn't possibly care if we swam in it. We spent a very enjoyable hour "mud crawling" in that filthy pond before heading to the house. When Mom met us there I can't remember what she said , but I'm sure if I could I wouldn't be able to write it down. She reminded us that we were now going to have to try to get cleaned up to go to Bible school.

We had to bathe in a large tub out back of the house. I don't think we were able to get very clean and I know we couldn't get rid of the smell. We didn't really care at our ages about unimportant things like that. If I could go back in time, I'd like to see the faces of the teachers and other kids that day when we went to Bible school.

The smell from our "mud crawling adventure" must have lasted for a week.

After that, we were allowed to swim in the deep ponds and rivers by ourselves. I'm not sure if it was because they knew we were really good swimmers and could probably take care of ourselves, or they just didn't want to risk us going back to that stinking pond again.

My favorite part of school during those years was summer vacation, as you can probably tell by now. The summers went by fast, and now we were back in school. The subjects I liked best were geography, math and anything that had to do with nature. I didn't like English or spelling. I always liked to read and read several times as many books as was required.

During those days the PTA meetings were attended by everyone in the community. They were like a major social event. Sometimes the teacher would have us present a program during these meetings. The program I remember most was when I was the patient on the operating table. Two of the other students were the doctors. They were arguing about if I had cancer or a tumor. One of the doctors reached in and pulled out "two more" and said see I told you it was tumor.

Everyone walked to school in those days. Some of the students had to walk as far as three miles. I was disappointed that we lived so close to school and I didn't have to walk very far. At times, I even walked part way with them and then back home by myself. One day three of the younger girls decided to take a shortcut across a muddy field on their way to school. One of them made it to school and told us her two younger sisters were stuck in the mud out in the middle of that field. Two of us older boys and the father of some of the other students had to go carry them out of the mud. They were only going to save a few minutes and it took us half an hour to get them out.

One of the guys in school grew up faster than the rest of us. He always had to prove that he could whip the rest of us every year when school started. During the summer, between my seventh and eighth grades, I helped put up several thousand square and little round bales of hay. Looking back I guess that's why when he tried to whip me when we started the eighth grade, I was much stronger than he was. That was the last time we fought.

During those years I had several girlfriends. Of course, I was too bashful to let them know I liked them. There was one particular girl that I really liked. I always managed to sit in the desk behind her. Back then we had box or pie suppers where the girls would put a meal for two in a decorated box for the guys to bid on. I remember one year being outbid on the box supper of that girl I really liked. I was devastated and vowed to not let that happen again. The next year I bought the box supper she brought. We went out and sat in a car and ate our meals. We didn't say much, and I was disgusted with myself for being so shy. After Kincaid closed, we kind of drifted our separate ways. While in high school when I broke up with a girl I was going steady with, she came and talked to me as a friend, trying to help. Looking back now, I think she must have known that I really liked her back in those days in that old country school.

    I was in the last eighth grade class to graduate from Kincaid school in the spring of 1956. School districts were being consolidated, and within a few years all the old one room country schools were closed. The land went back to the farm on our home place. My Dad bought the schoolhouse, and my wife Connie and I now own the home place and the Old Country School.

Chapter 4

To Grandma and Grandpa's House

I used to enjoy going to my Grandma and Grandpa Couch's house to stay for a few days at a time. Grandpa and I both liked to hunt and fish. When we would go fishing, he would sit for hours with his cane pole in the same spot. It didn't matter to him if the fish were biting or not, as he seemed to be enjoying himself one way or the other.

I, on the other hand, didn't have that much patience. I'd move from place to place hoping to find just the right spot where they were biting. Sometimes we caught a lot of fish and sometimes none, but it was always fun fishing with Grandpa.

Grandpa raised a big garden with lots of watermelons. When they got ripe, he would always have several in the shade to cool out in the yard by his favorite bench. Whenever we were there, he'd always ask us to sit out in the yard and he would cut a watermelon for us to eat. Just when we started eating it he'd say, "let's cut another one, maybe it will be better." The one we were eating was good, but it didn't matter to him. He'd just cut another one anyway. He would end up cutting four or five before he was satisfied, just to make sure we were eating one of the best ones he had raised. Grandpa would always cut way more watermelons than we could possibly eat.

In the late summer, Grandpa and I would squirrel hunt in the woods north of their house. I always liked to climb trees when we would hunt together. I'd climb a hickory that was just the right size to "ride down ." When I had climbed to where it was small enough, it would bend down completely to the ground where I'd get off. Then it would suddenly whip back straight up like a slingshot. Grandpa always said that I "could climb a thorn tree one hundred feet high with a wildcat under each arm and never get a scratch." I'm not sure who was prouder, him telling that story about me to someone, or me listening to him tell it.

One day I climbed up in a big oak tree that was hollow. When I looked inside, there was a big coon in it looking back at me. I decided to try and get him out of there. I kept poking on him until he started to climb out. All of a sudden out he came, almost knocking me out of the tree as he passed within inches in his desperate attempt to escape. He jumped the twenty feet or more to the ground where Grandpa's old dog was waiting for him. The old dog was no match for that big old coon and he soon got away.

The quail were really thick back then. I remember hunting them without a bird dog and having good hunts because they were so thick. Where there is one covey now with fifteen birds, there were probably ten coveys back then with twenty birds in each one.

During the winter when there was snow on the ground, we'd go rabbit hunting. That was my least favorite thing to hunt. I didn't care much about eating them either. After a cold day hunting rabbits, I'd head into Grandma and Grandpa's kitchen and lie on the cot between the wood cook stove and the wall. It was so warm and cozy there that I would fall into an instant sleep.

Grandma and Grandpa both passed away several years ago. The farm is not the same now as it was when I was a boy and would visit for a few days. The house caught fire and burned down, and the woods are now open pasture. But in my mind, I can still see that old house. Grandma is inside baking her famous homemade light rolls that always filled the house with a delicious smell. Outside, there on his favorite bench beside the house, Grandpa sits, cutting another watermelon, with me by his side eating away.

Chapter 5

A Crop of My Own

When I was around ten years old, Dad decided to let me grow a crop on a small field on the north side of our farm. It was about an acre in size surrounded by woods. After thinking about the crops I could grow for a while, I decided to plant it in popcorn. I was excited to finally get my field planted that spring. It came up and looked great all summer long. The only thing I hadn't counted on was all the squirrels that lived in those woods loved corn.

Each time I went to check out my popcorn, I would discover that the squirrels had eaten some more of it. I began to wonder if I was going to have any left by the time it was ready to shuck.

When the corn got mature enough to shuck, I was relieved to see that the squirrels had only eaten the corn from the outside rows. I shucked all the corn by hand and stored it in a shed to finish drying.

Usually, when we shelled the popcorn we grew for our own use, we did it by hand. However, now I had several bushels of popcorn to shell and hand shelling seemed to be out of the question. We had an old hand crank corn sheller that I tried to use for a while, but that seemed too slow as well. I decided to try to mount an electric motor on that old sheller and to every ones surprise's, including me, it actually worked great! After that, it didn't take very long to get it shelled with the rig I had fixed up.

When the wind was blowing just right, I got it all aired out by pouring it from one container to another. This let the wind blow the lighter chaff away, while the heaver grains of popcorn went into the other container. This turned out to be harder work than getting it shelled. I would work at it until I was worn out for that day, and then start again the next time the wind was blowing. It took me several days to get it all done.

Chapter 5 - A CROP OF MY OWN

Soon it was time to market all that popcorn. Dad drove me to some kind of distribution center for groceries in Hannibal, Missouri, where we thought we would be able to sell all of it. He let me do most of the talking, even though I didn't have a clue what I was doing. The story they told us was that they didn't buy fresh popcorn. It had to be aged for a year before they would even consider it. That seemed rather strange to us, as we had raised popcorn for our own use for as long as I could remember, and it was always best the first year. We wondered if that was just an excuse they used in order to get rid of us.

After that big disappointment, Dad drove me to several grocery stores where I managed to sell some of my popcorn. I was also able to sell some of it to several individuals. I didn't have very much expense in that crop out of my own pocket, so the eighty some dollars I made looked huge to me at that time.

When I had sold all I could, I started giving it away to friends and neighbors. We still had more popcorn left than we could use that year. I've planted popcorn off and on for years after that for our own use. But even though it was a great experience, I vowed to never again go to all the work it took to raise that acre of popcorn.

Chapter 6

The Town of Warren

The town of Warren is in the west central area of Marion County Missouri about twenty five miles west of Hannibal. It was first settled in the mid 1800's.

My Granny Thurman told me that when she was a girl during the late 1800's and early 1900's, there was a shoe factory, a hotel and a blacksmith shop in Warren, in addition to several stores. In those days, their transportation was by horse and buggy, so long distances for weekly supplies was out of the question. When she was a girl, farms were much smaller than they are today and there was a higher percentage of the population living in the rural areas. There was a store every four or five miles during those days in this area.

Railroads were a very important form of shipment and transportation in the mid to late eighteen hundreds. It was thought that a railroad would eventually go through the town of Warren, so the town grew. In 1851 construction began on a railroad from Hannibal, Missouri to St Joseph, Missouri. It went through the towns of Palmyra and Monroe City, but didn't go through the town of Warren. After that, the town of Warren stopped growing for a number of years. Then in the early to mid nineteen hundreds, businesses started closing and the population gradually declined to approximately twenty people at the time of this writing in 2012. There are no businesses in Warren anymore, but there are still a few homes, and the Baptist church still holds services each Sunday.

There were still two stores in Warren when I was a young boy. The O'Bryan store, which had been there for years, was on the corner. The Burditt store, which was newer and more modern inside, was right beside it.

When I got old enough, I would ride my bike around two and a half miles to Warren to buy a bottle of soda pop. The road was all gravel hauled from the gravel bars along the rivers in the area. There was a big hill to climb on the way there and another one to climb on the way back home. A bottle of soda only cost five cents at that time. My favorite flavors of soda were grapette and root beer, By the time I rode my bike back home, I'd be just as thirsty as when I started, but they sure were good.

    I enjoyed going to the O'Bryan store, as there was always something interesting to discover there. On the shelves sat old button shoes that no one wore anymore, their black color barely visible under the thick layers of dust that had collected for an unknown number of years. Old coal oil lamps from the era before electricity came to our rural area, stood high on a shelf, like sentinels in formation guarding their domain. Jars of old unwrapped hard rock candy sat on the counter untouched. A few old rusty guns sat in the corner, along with ammunition of various brands. Each time I was there, I would examine each one as though it were a treasure of great value.

    You could buy groceries, clothes, shoes, and other supplies in both stores. The O'Bryan store had what appeared to be an old church pew in the corner by the wood heating stove. A few wooden chairs, worn from years of use, sat on both sides in no particular order.

During the coldest days of winter after they finished feeding their livestock, men from the neighborhood would sometimes gather there to visit. Among them were a few retired old timers, who passed the long hours there almost every day. Whenever I got the chance, I'd listen to the stories they told for hours at a time. Some of the stories told by the old timers were from back in the 1800's. I remember thinking how I wished I had been born back at that time, since I was fascinated by the history and events of that era.

During that time, there was also a telephone switchboard in Warren. I remember going into the small room in the back of Dutch McCormick's house to watch him make the connections for each call that was made. Everyone had a certain ring on their old crank phones to call on their own line, but if you wanted to call someone on another line, you had to go through the switchboard in Warren.

My Dad told me several things about Warren and interesting events that took place there before my time. He said that during the depression he would walk across country to Warren, shooting rabbits on the way. At that time, you could sell rabbits to be shipped to the big cities for food. He would sell the rabbits at the O'Bryan store and use the money he got for them to buy supplies for the coming week. He said the rabbits were thrown in a barrel for shipment just as they were brought in. How those people that ate those rabbits kept from getting food poisoning, I'll never know. As Dad walked back across country on the way home, he'd shoot some more rabbits for the family to eat.

Another story Dad told me about Warren was about a group of men in the O'Bryan store that decided to have a cracker eating contest. The object was to see who could eat the most crackers without drinking anything. Anyway, Dad said they ran out of crackers and decided to finish the contest by substituting flour for the crackers. He said the contest ended pretty quickly after that. I can't imagine why can you?

There are two springs near Warren that never run dry. The closest one is about three fourths of a mile down the gravel road south of Warren. It flows out of a small cave at the bottom of a rocky bluff, and is just big enough for a grown man to crawl into. Some of the old

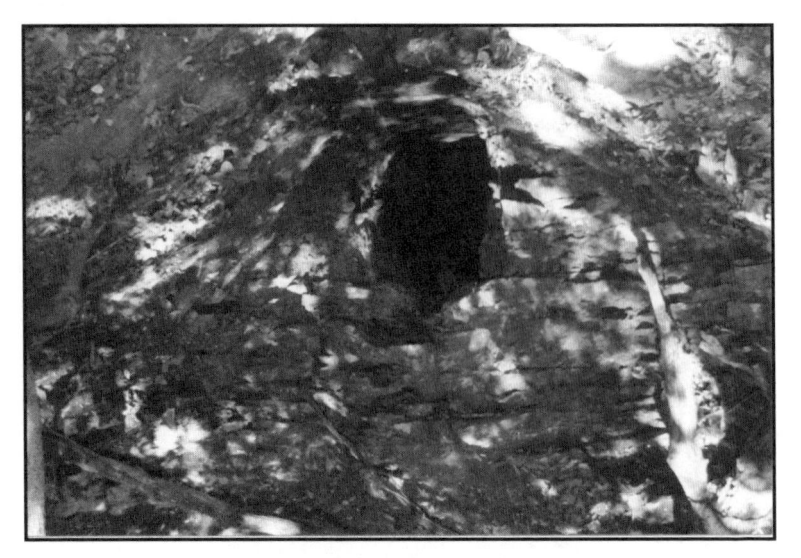

The cave spring south of Warren.

timers told stories of someone going way back in that cave. They said there were large rooms toward the back of the cave, beyond the narrow passageways. I never was sure if they were telling the truth, or if they were just tall tales they made up. I thought about exploring it for myself several times, but never did. There were a lot of copperhead snakes in that area, and somehow the idea of being in close quarters with one of them kept me from ever making that exploration trip. When I was growing up, someone was always talking about exploring it, but as far as I know no one ever did.

    The other spring was about four miles south of Warren on the side of a hill by the South River bottoms. Someone had built a rock springhouse over it. On hot summer days when Dad and I would be fishing along the river, I'd start thinking about that cold crystal clear water from that spring. We would always stop there when we were finished fishing, and it was the best water I had ever tasted. I looked forward to drinking that cold spring water almost as much as I looked forward to our fishing trips.

Dad said during the drought years of the 1930's, wells and cisterns went dry in the area, but those two springs just kept flowing. He said people came from miles around to replenish their water supplies from those springs. In my mind, I can picture horse drawn wagons loaded with wooden barrels being filled with water dipped from those two springs, while poor children from that depression era played in the cold streams below them.

There is a huge soapstone bluff southeast of Warren that some of my friends and I decided we would try to climb one day. The rocks on the steep slope were the color aqua, and slick just like soap. They were about the size of a cake of soap you would throw away. You couldn't get a foothold on them, as they would slide out from under you as soon as you put any weight on them. The bluff was around one hundred and fifty feet high, and the higher you got the steeper it got. At the top of the slope there was an overhang of about twenty feet. Two of us finally managed to climb to the top of the main slope by going up where the water from a wet weather waterfall had cut a small ditch. We made several attempts to get up the overhang and finally realized we weren't going to be able to reach the top without some ropes. How we kept from falling in our attempts to climb up over that overhang I'll never know. If we had fallen from it, we wouldn't have been able to stop until we reached the bottom of the bluff. We had planned to go back with ropes but never did, which was probably a good thing!

The O'bryan Store in Warren Missouri, around 100 years ago.

Chapter
7

My Sister Beth

Beth and Me on the Pourch

My sister Ada Elizabeth (Beth) was born in 1948, six years younger than me. She claims I managed to convince her to do all the tasks that I needed help with, without much of a reward afterward. Looking back, I guess she was probably right.

I had learned to make rope by twisting several strands of baler twine until it wanted to twist back on itself. That was the secret. All you had to do then was to go to the center of the twisted strands and hold on there, while letting it have some slack. It would twist on itself and make a rope that looked just like rope that was manufactured. The worst part about this method was that it was so slow, so I figured out a way to tie the strands of twine to the rear wheel of my bicycle. I turned the bike upside down and turned the pedals by hand to twist the strands of twine. I decided it was working so well that I'd make a lot of rope, but I'd need lots of help. That's when I decided to recruit my sister to help. I'm not sure if she thought it was a privilege to help her big brother at the time, or was just really gullible, but she was always willing to help. We collected all the used twine that we could find around the barns and sheds until we had several hundred feet. After I got it all tied to the bike wheel and ready for the twisting I assigned Beth the job of turning the pedals on the bike.

Chapter 7 - MY SISTER BETH

My sister Beth and me with the bike we used to make rope.

    You can probably imagine how long it took to turn those pedals to make that much rope. I always figured anything worth doing was worth doing in a big way, and that certainly applied to the amount of rope we were making. After we had made enough rope to scale a large mountain, I contrived a method of fashioning a rope ladder to enable me to climb into my tree house. While I was making the ladder, Beth watched, with every muscle in her body sore from all that cranking she had done. When I completed the ladder, it resembled something even Tarzan would have been proud of. As I made my first ascent into the tree house, Beth patiently waited below for her turn. Just as she reached for the ladder, I pulled it up just out of reach of her outstretched arms. As she looked up at me, the hurt and disappointment was plain to see. However being the typical brother, I continued to pull the ladder up to my platform. Why did she think I had made the ladder from rope anyway? I guess I must have had an ornery streak in me back then, as this had been my plan all along. After a few days, I began to feel guilty and let her use the rope ladder to climb into the tree house with me. I was getting bored sitting in it by myself anyway. The way I remember the experience, it turned out to be more fun when we both played in it after that. It wasn't long however, before I had moved on to some new adventure and we both abandoned the tree house forever. The way it turned out, we spent a lot more time making the tree house and the ladder than actually using it.

One fall day when Beth was small, she went with Dad and me to cut down some trees for our winter's wood supply. I had a brand new hatchet that was very sharp. Beth begged me to use it to cut down a tree of her own. I didn't want her to use it, but then Dad said "go on and let her have it, she can't hurt it any!" I didn't have much choice after that, so I reluctantly handed it to her. She started hacking away on a small tree as Dad and I continued cutting up logs for our wood. After a while, we noticed Beth had stopped cutting down the tree she had been working on. She was just standing there looking as if she was trying to hide something. Dad went over to see what was wrong and saw that she had blood on her jeans. The hatchet had glanced off the tree she was cutting and sliced right through her jeans into the middle of her knee. She says she learned a lesson about sharp blades that day, and she still has a scar on that knee.

There was a huge old fashioned barn on the farm when Beth and I were growing up. It had been built in the eighteen hundreds and had horse stalls on one side and cattle and sheep sheds on the other side. In the center of the barn there was a raised hallway with a corn crib and an oat bin to one side of it. It had a large hayloft that was originally used to store loose hay.

During the 1950's when Beth and I were growing up, it was being used to store square bales of hay. The floor of the loft had deteriorated from age and from all the tons of hay that had been piled on it over the years. Dad decided the loft floor was only strong enough to put four layers of square bales on it. Beth and I made an intricate system of tunnels and rooms all over the loft underneath those bales. We spent many enjoyable hours designing, building, changing, and playing in those tunnels and rooms. Every spring, Beth was usually the first to find a new nest of kittens that the mother cat had tucked away in a well hidden spot in the loft. She would spend hours playing with those kittens until they followed her everywhere. When it came time to give them away, she would always have a very hard time parting with any of them,

One hot summer day, we had a bad storm with a heavy downpour. We always knew when that happened the water gaps across the Big Branch on the north forty would be washed out. The north forty was on a separate part of the farm that was about three miles from where we lived. Dad had tied four strands of barbed wire across the Big Branch on both sides of our land. He called these strands the water gaps. The barbed wires were connected to our fence on each side of the Big Branch, with strong wire on one side and light weight wire on the other side.

This let it wash out, without damaging the entire fence. All that needed to be done to put it back up was to tie it back where it had washed loose from the power of the rushing water. This sounds easy, but the wires were usually all tangled up with limbs, and it would sometimes take two or three hours of hard work to get them back in place. When Dad thought we had waited long enough for the water to go down in the Big Branch, he said we needed to go put the water gaps back up before the cows got out.

It was usually fun going to the north forty because there was about twenty acres of bluffs and woods along the Big Branch to explore. However, as hot and humid as it was that day I wasn't looking forward to going and was really surprised when Beth said she wanted to go along. When we got there, sure enough both gaps were washed out. While we were working putting the gaps back up, Dad and Beth were continually swatting at mosquitoes. They were all around me too and were an aggravation, but they weren't biting me at all.

When we finally got finished, we were all drenched in sweat and were ready to head for home. After we all got cleaned up, Dad and Beth both had welts all over them from all the mosquito bites they had gotten. They couldn't believe that I didn't have a single mosquito bite on me anywhere. Seems like they kidded me saying something like, "guess you were so rotten the mosquitoes didn't even want to eat on you!"

Chapter 8

Skunks

Most people hate the smell of skunks however, I think they smell good. I know that sounds strange to most people, but here's the rest of the story. When I was growing up, my Granny Thurman lived in the same house we did during the summer. She stayed in two rooms, which left my Mom and Dad, Beth and me two bedrooms, a kitchen and a living room to share.

One year when I was ten or eleven years old, my parents bought a new rug for the living room floor. I decided to put the old rug to good use by making some sort of a tent out of it. We had two big cedar trees in our back yard that were about fifteen feet apart, and the rug was twelve feet square. I tied a rope between the trees and hung the rug over it under side out to shed water. I was pretty proud of myself as it made a great tent, even though it was open on both ends.

I found an old iron bed frame with cross wires to hold up a mattress that Mom had decided to throw away and put it in my homemade tent. I got some blankets and I was ready to try out my "new home" for the night. That one night turned into the whole summer, as I loved it out there. It also helped the whole family because we weren't short a bedroom like we had been the last few summers.

My "new home" had a lot of advantages. It cooled out much faster than it did in the house because both ends were open. I was pretty much on my own when I was out there and I liked that as well. From the time I was small, I can't remember ever being afraid of being alone or afraid of the dark, so that didn't bother me either.

I remember one moonlit night when it was so hot I couldn't sleep, so I decided to go for a walk and ended up down by the river bridge over two miles from home. It's a good thing Mom and Dad didn't decide to check on me that night. They wouldn't

Chapter 8 - SKUNKS

have had any way of knowing I was just fine, and would have worried for nothing. I went for several long walks at night after that, and no one ever knew about it until now.

When a storm would come up, Dad would come out to where I was sleeping and I can still hear him say, "Don't you think you better come in?" I never did want to go in, but sometimes he made me anyway. Years later a storm blew the top out of one of those trees and it fell right where my tent had been. "Sometimes parents know best."

Now back to why I like the smell of skunks. My two dogs were always catching skunks and getting sprayed. They slept under that old bed most nights, so you can you imagine how strong the skunk smell was under that old rug. At first it seemed pretty terrible, but I guess this proves you can get used to almost anything because after a while it didn't seem so bad. After a month or two, if it wasn't too strong, I actually began to like it. Anyway now every time I smell a skunk I think back in time to that summer I spent sleeping under that old rug in our backyard. In my mind, I'm sleeping on that old bed with those two dogs under it smelling just like a skunk.

It was such a simple thing at the time, but now the memories it brings back are priceless.

Years later after Dad had passed on and Mom was still living alone on the home place, she had a very unusual experience with skunks. She didn't get out much during the winter and early spring as she was in her eighties and was afraid of falling. However, she had several cats that she fed just outside the north porch door each day. One day when she was feeding her cats, a skunk showed up. At first it stayed back in the distance until she would go back in the house. Then when she was out of sight, it would actually come and eat out of the bowls right beside the cats. It gradually got used to Mom, and after a few days it would come and eat with the cats while she was only a few feet away. This in itself seemed unusual, but there was something even more unusual yet to come.

As she fed the cats on a warm day during that spring, the skunk showed up with a whole litter of baby skunks. Mom would wait patiently each day hoping they would show up again, and they usually did. After a few days, they became even more gentle than their mother had been and soon they were also eating with the cats. Each day, Mom would stand a little closer to where they were eating until she was right there beside them. They had gotten so used to her that they didn't pay any attention to her at all. One day, Mom reached down and petted one of the baby skunks while it was eating there with her cats. A few days later, they disappeared into the wild never to be seen again. Neither I, nor anyone else I have told about this, have ever heard of anyone petting a wild skunk.

    As I think back about this, I wonder why I didn't take the time to go with a camera and get a picture of Mom with those skunks. It was during the busy time on the farm when I was putting in our crops, but now it would be an easy decision to give up the gain I made that day for just one picture of Mom petting that baby skunk.

Chapter
9

The Buzzards Nest

It is the spring of 1954. I am twelve years old and full of adventure. Dad and I are winding along a dirt road each of us driving 9N Ford tractors. Dad is in the lead and I'm following. Huge oak trees mixed with hickories and maples are so thick that the sunlight seldom reaches the ground. Redbuds and wild flowers are scattered in a few of the more open areas. The warmth of the sun feels good melting away the memories of the cold winter, just as it did the snows that had blanketed the land not long ago.

The road is becoming steeper as it winds along the side of one of the huge bluffs in the area. It has a rough rocky surface and a dangerous drop-off on one

The Road to the Field

side. It becomes necessary to shift into low gear in order to descend to the big creek we'll have to cross to reach the field we intend to plow. When we reach the creek we see we have another problem. The rains have washed a huge sandbar into the only crossing. Dad is probably wondering why we ever agreed to farm this field about now. As he drives his small Ford into the sand, I'm sure he'll get stuck. I see his tractor sinking into the quicksand like surface ahead of me as I wait for my turn. Just when I'm sure he's stuck, he surges ahead and reaches the other side.

After watching Dad get across, I'm hoping I won't be disgraced by getting stuck. In my mind I'm already somewhat

Chapter 9 - THE BUZZARDS NEST

of an expert tractor driver. I wouldn't want it to get out that Dad was able to make the crossing but I couldn't. It is now or never, so I surge ahead. About midway across, I start sinking. The sand and water come clear up to the Ford tractors axels and my forward progress has almost ceased. Just when I'm sure there is no way I'm going to make it, I realize I'm no longer sinking. The crossing has a solid rock slab under it that prevents me from sinking any deeper, so I now continue spinning my way across. As I reach the other side I realize with relief that my expert driver reputation is safe.

The field looks huge to my twelve year old eyes. It is irregular shaped in such a way that I can't even see all of it from our vantage point. Its slopes look almost too steep to farm. Dad says its forty seven acres. I'm beginning to dread having to plow all this with our two small plows. Each of our plows that we use to turn the soil only till twenty eight inches in each pass we make across the field.

After I've plowed a few hours, I can't stand it any longer. I've been plotting how I'm going to ask Dad to let me explore the area ever since we started. I'm surprised when he says I can look the area over for an hour or two. Even though I'm only twelve he knows I won't get lost as I've been exploring unknown areas by myself for several years.

    The woods are alive with the songs of birds and the chatter of squirrels as they obviously are enjoying this beautiful spring day. When I reach the area where a bluff drops towards the creek below, I see that I'll have to go around a rock ledge in order to get down to the creek. Not wanting to go around I decide I can climb over it instead. As I climb down the steep rocky ledge a buzzard suddenly flies from under it. As I look under the ledge I'm surprised to see three large cream colored eggs there among the rocks against the back wall. I decided not to get any closer since I wanted the female buzzard to come back. I'm already looking forward to coming back to discover if the eggs hatch.

    As we go back to the field several days later to prepare it for planting I can hardly wait to check on the eggs. I'm relieved to see the female buzzard fly from under the ledge as I approach the cliff. As I climb back to where I can see the eggs I'm not prepared for what I'm about to see. I carefully work my way down where I can get a good look. There under the ledge are three fluffy, snow white,

Chapter 9 - THE BUZZARDS NEST

The Ledge where I found the baby buzzard nest.

cute as can be, little buzzards. I can hardly believe that they are the young of such ugly parents. Up close adult turkey buzzards are about the ugliest birds I know of. However when you watch them fly, riding the thermals high in the sky, they are beautiful in flight.

Each time I returned to work in the field the first thing I did was to go see the little buzzards. I was amazed at how fast they were growing. When they started getting their feathers, the cute was leaving and the ugly was beginning to show up.

As spring was giving into summer, I was making my way over the ledge to check them out again. As I approached the area with my usual anticipation, I wasn't prepared for what was about to happen. When I got close to them, they started making a hissing noise . I kept moving closer to get a better look, since I knew it wouldn't be long before they would be able to fly. When I got about twelve feet from them, they vomited all that foul smelling carrion their parents had brought them! This was their way of protecting themselves from a threat, but it smelled so bad I almost lost everything I had eaten before I could get out of there. That was the last time I saw them. I had no desire to go back after that.

    Now many years later, I can still see Dad and me going down through those woods towards that field on those two Ford tractors. The huge oaks are still there. The bluffs and hills remain the same. Dad has passed on and times have made many changes. But my memories of those times in the past are as vivid as if they were only yesterday. We can never go back to those times from our past, but I still have many fond memories of those little white buzzards and the year I watched them.

    I sometimes wonder if buzzards are still laying their eggs under that ledge; If each spring the eggs hatch and there

Chapter 9 - THE BUZZARDS NEST

are downy white as new-fallen snow little buzzards waiting there for some adventurous young boy to discover them, just as I did many years ago.

Chapter
10

Discoveries in the Wild

From the time I was able to walk I have always been intrigued by nature. As a young boy, I would spend hours around ponds observing and catching live frogs and turtles. I developed a method of catching frogs that was almost foolproof. First, I'd walk around the bank and make several frogs jump in the water. They would come up after a while out in the middle of the pond. All I had to do was watch which direction one was headed, and when he went under to swim towards the bank, I'd run towards where I thought he was going to come up. When he surfaced near the edge of the water, I'd be waiting. I'd grab him before he even knew I was there. You had to be patient and you had to be quick, but I got so good at it that I seldom missed. I also caught several turtles each year by hand. I had a big cattle tank, out by our windmill, where I kept my turtles. They were mostly snapping turtles with an occasional soft shelled turtle. I had put boards in the water for them to climb on to sun themselves. When we dressed our frying chickens, I'd give them the chicken guts, They loved them. "Yum."

We had a neighbor that owned a pet raccoon named Rascal. I can't remember for sure how they got him, but it seems like they found him after a bad storm when he was small. He grew to be a big rascal, and was full of mischief. I remember spending many enjoyable days playing with him down by a small spring fed creek that ran by just south of their house. It was littered with rocks of all shapes and sizes. There were crawdads under some of the flat rocks in the shallow water. As I would turn the rocks over, Rascal would watch intently for them. He was an expert at catching them and seldom missed. Before he would eat the crawdads, he would wash them between his front paws just like a human would have washed them between their hands. Kids today have computers,

TV's, cell phones, ipods, and all kinds of other high-tech devices, but how many will ever have a pet raccoon to play with? I wouldn't want to give up those things now, but I'm glad I didn't have them back then, since I might have missed out on most of the outdoor fun and adventures in the outdoors during my youth.

I decided I wanted to be a trapper when I was in grade school. I set out a few old used traps not far from our house where I could check them each morning before going to school. I don't remember catching much, but the one thing I do remember catching was a great horned owl. I carefully removed him from the trap and carried him to our house to show my parents. As I carried him, he would occasionally spread his wings in an attempt to fly. I was amazed at how wide his wingspan was and also for what appeared to be a big bird how little he weighed. They couldn't believe the owl hadn't tried to peck my eyes out, as I had carried him upright by his feet with his beak close to my head. The old traps I had used didn't have much power and the owl appeared not to be injured. I took him back up towards where I had caught him and set him free. This may sound strange, but ever since then I have felt somehow connected to owls. After that I gave up on the idea of being a trapper and took up all my traps.

I was always trying to catch something by hand and my next challenge was to catch a full grown rabbit. I had caught several small rabbits, but I knew that didn't really count because they were so easy to catch. Dad watched me try to run down or sneak up on several rabbits and said I was wasting my time. But he probably already knew I wasn't going to give up that easy. One day I chased a big rabbit under our outhouse. I couldn't reach him through the cracks in the floor, so I decided to take up a board to get to him. I ended up tearing most of the floor out of our outhouse before I finally caught him. It never entered my mind that a rabbit could hurt you, but I learned they could that day. I was on my way to show Dad that I had caught a grown rabbit by hand when it gave a kick with one of its hind legs. Its toenail caught my arm and left a welt-like scratch the whole length of my forearm. So I got two rewards that day for catching a full grown rabbit: a painful scratch and into trouble for tearing the floor out of our outhouse. While I was replacing the floor that day, all Dad said was, "What were you thinking?"

Chapter 10 - DISCOVERIES IN THE WILD

I always liked to go mushroom hunting each spring. One year around the last of April we had a lot of rain and it turned really warm, which was the ideal condition for mushrooms. I decided to go on one of our Ford tractors to the back side of our Home Place where several large elm trees had died the year before. I headed straight for two of the biggest dead elms along a fence row, where our farm bordered the farm to the north of it. When I reached them, to my amazement there appeared to be hundreds of the biggest mushrooms I had ever seen under those old trees. I had only taken a few bread sacks with me, and I quickly filled all of them. I didn't want to go back to the house for more sacks, so I took off my shirt, tied knots in the sleeves and buttoned it up, making a fairly large sack out of it. When I got that full, I took off my hat and filled it. I had finally picked all the mushrooms under those two trees, but I still had to get them to the house. The weight wasn't as much of a problem as the bulk of all those bags and everything else I had put them into. I finally got them on the tractor and got them back to our house where everyone was amazed at how many I had found. We put them in a washtub to wash and cut up as it was the only container that was big enough to hold all of them at once. I told everyone that I had found so many mushrooms under two trees that it took a tractor to haul them out of the woods, which was the truth in a way. We ate mushrooms that spring until we were tired of them, and even gave some of them away so we wouldn't have to eat them. I've hunted mushrooms every year since then and have never found that many again in one day, or even in a whole season. Maybe someday we'll have another spring where all the conditions will be ideal again, and I'll find another bunch of mushrooms like I did that spring so long ago.

When I was a freshman in high school, I rode the bus every day. As we were going through Rocky Hollow one spring evening on the way home from school, I saw several small foxes playing near a hole under a big rock from the window of the bus. My cousin and I decided to try to catch one of them for a pet. Our plan was that I would sneak in and wait by the hole. My cousin would chase them toward me, where I would catch one of them as he tried to escape in the hole under the rock. We both wore leather gloves to keep them from biting us. I ran for the hole when they saw me, and although some of them that were close to their den and were able to beat me there, not all of them made it. When my cousin ran after one of them, it ran for its den just as we had expected it to. That little fox was quick and hard to catch, but we finally caught it. For a while it was hard to tell who had who, as it was a lot bigger than we had thought and it fought us for its life. We should have let it go right then, as it was obvious it was too old and too big for us to ever make it gentle enough for a pet. However, we were young and had decided we were going to have a pet fox, so we took it home. We put it in a " break up coop" which was a large screened in cage where Mom put the hens that wanted to sit on the eggs. Our fox was a wild animal that was going to stay wild no matter what we did, and it didn't get any calmer. One day when I was trying to calm it down by petting it, I got bit for my trouble. Mom said she needed her break up coop for some hens, so my cousin took it to their farm and put it in a wood corn crib. I never saw that poor little fox again and I'm not sure what happened to it. I learned a lesson from it though. "Some things in the wild should remain there."

Chapter 11

The Car Hood Boat

When I was about fourteen, I decided I needed a boat. I had imagined myself floating down raging rivers in a beautiful sleek boat. At other times, I would think of myself catching a world record fish from my boat while others watched in envy from the bank. I only had one thing in the way of my big plans at that time. I didn't have enough money to buy the kind of boat I wanted.

Then, one day as Dad drove by a house about ten miles from our home, I spotted a for sale sign on something that looked almost like a boat. I got Dad to stop for a look and we found out that someone had welded two deep car hoods together in the form of a boat. Well, this wasn't what I had in mind, but it was cheap and I ended up buying it.

They made cars from heavy metal in those days, and the weight of that old boat was more than I could carry by myself. I purchased a canoe paddle and made another one out of a board to save money. When we finally got it in the water, I was amazed at how it handled just like those high priced boats I had dreamed about.

I used that old boat for all the things I had dreamed of doing with a fancy boat over the next several years. I remember catching lots of fish out of the rivers in our area from inside that old boat, even though I never came close to that world record fish I had imagined myself catching.

Some of my friends and I used it to float and camp on the rivers in our area. I remember one float trip a friend and I took really well. It was during a dry spell in the month of August. We had someone drop us, the old boat, and all our gear off at a bridge on North River where we began our float trip. Over the next two days, we planned to float down the river to another bridge several miles away.

Chapter 11 - THE CAR HOOD BOAT

It didn't take long for us to realize this wasn't going to be an easy float trip like we had planned on. The river was extremely low and where we were usually able to float over all the rifles, we were now having to carry everything. We tried dragging the boat through a few of them, but we soon realized the gravel was going to wear a hole in the bottom of the boat if we kept doing that. So, now we were carrying the boat and our gear about as much as we were floating. It was hot and we were miserable! We soon ran out of water, so we drank right out of the river. We were either tough or just lucky because neither one of us got sick from drinking it. We were soon wishing we had never decided to go on this float trip. We had no way of contacting anyone, so we just struggled on, knowing we were going to have to work hard in order to make it to our pickup point in two days.

We had planned to catch fish for most of our meals, and this soon proved to be another problem, as the fish just about refused to bite. We both said we were wondering what would go wrong next. We finally managed to catch a few fish for our evening meal. They were cleaned and prepared using the river water. We fried them in an iron skillet over an open campfire that night, and I don't ever remember any fish that tasted as good as those did. After using sand and river water to clean our skillet, we rolled up in our old army blankets for the night. As I listened to the owls and felt the coolness of the night breeze, everything began to seem well with the world as I drifted off to sleep.

The next thing I knew, it was beginning to get light. I had been so tired I hadn't moved all night. We ate what little food we had brought with us and headed for the bridge, still several miles on down the river, where we hoped to be picked up, if our timing was right.

The second day was pretty much the same as the first one, except we were tiring out more quickly from lugging that heavy boat and all our gear so much. We were so hungry we were sure we could eat a whole steer, if we ever got the chance! Finally, we saw the bridge in the distance. Seeing it seemed to give us a surge of strength and it didn't take us long to get to it, where someone was waiting for us. It seems strange that even though this float trip was the hardest one I ever went on, it's the one I remember the most about.

Chapter 11 - THE CAR HOOD BOAT

The old car hood boat began to rust through the last few years I had it. I'd patch one hole, only to have it start leaking in another spot the next time I would use it. I finally gave up on it and just left it to rust away, never to be used again. Now when I think back about that old thing I first saw along the road, I realize how much it meant to me for the fifteen years I used it. It had been a good old boat!

Chapter

12

Dogs

For as long as I can remember I have always had one or more dogs. When I was three years old, my cousin Judy gave me a Rat Terrier puppy that I named Spot. Later, I had a black and white long-haired dog I called Frisky. When I was a teenager, a Collie crossed with a German Shepherd dog showed up at our farm. We called him Spike. He could run like a Greyhound, and both my Dad and I saw him at different times run down and catch a fox. He loved to hunt and could tree more squirrels than any dog I had ever seen. There was just one problem, he was gun shy. If you had a gun with you he would abandon the tree just before you got there. While I still had Spike, I bought a Treeing Walker Coonhound named Joe.

I started hunting coons with a neighbor named Henry Rhodes after I got out of High School. He had a Redbone Coonhound and I had old Joe. One year, we got sixty six coons. We skinned all of them and stretched the skins on boards, which was a lot of work. I still have a picture of Henry and me with all those coons and our two dogs lined up beside a white board fence by Henry's house. The price for coon skins dropped that year and we only got one dollar and thirty five cents for each one. But the memories of those hunts we shared that year are priceless.

After Henrys health began to fail, I hunted coons for a year or two by myself with old Joe and Spike. I spent many a lonely night hunting alone way into the night because none of my friends cared anything about coon hunting.

I always had a good sense of direction and thought it was impossible for me to get lost, and then one night it happened. I was hunting in an area that I thought I knew fairly well and wasn't paying too much attention to where I was. Each time the dogs ran a coon, I ended up further from where I had parked my truck. I had

Chapter 12 - DOGS

Henry (right) and Me (left) with dogs and coon skins

gotten three big coons and was carrying them, along with two flashlights and a gun, which was a lot of weight, so I was ready to quit for the night. I started walking towards where I thought I had left the truck, but somehow things just didn't look right. After I had gotten the last coon, I had ended up in a grove of cedars that were so thick I could hardly walk through them. I knew I had never been there before, but I often hunted in places I was unfamiliar with, so that hadn't concerned me at the time. It was a cloudy night so I had nothing to go by except my sense of direction, which I was beginning to doubt. Anyway, I just kept walking in the direction where I thought my truck was parked. After about an hour of this, I came out on a gravel road that at first I didn't recognize. Then it hit me. I had walked west when I thought I was walking east and the road I had come out on was one I knew very well. The only problem I had now was that I had a long walk back around the road to where I had left my truck. I left the coons to be picked up later and headed for my truck. By the time I got home that night it was almost time to get up to feed the livestock. I can't remember if I even went to bed or not but I doubt it.

Another time when I went coon hunting by myself, I was lucky to have come back alive because of the foolish chance I took trying to get a coon. The dogs treed a coon up in a huge tree on the side of a rocky bluff. I had hunted hard that night and hadn't gotten a single coon, so I decided to climb that tree and see if there was a coon in the hole that was twenty or more feet from the ground. The tree was massive, with rough bark and a large bulge that appeared to be impossible to climb over, just below the hollow spot where I suspected the coon to be. I searched for limbs or handholds in hopes of finding a way to scale it's immense trunk, but there were none to be found. I had always said there wasn't a tree in the woods that I couldn't climb but this one didn't appear to be climbable. There was a smaller tree around eight or ten feet from it, so not wanting to give up I climbed the smaller tree to above the hole and bent it over to where I could jump onto the big tree.

Now I was really in big trouble even though I didn't realize it at the time. When I looked in the hole, sure enough I had been right as there was a big coon in it staring back at me. I poked him out and he jumped to the ground to where the dogs caught him. Then I started to evaluate my situation. Here I was twenty or more feet up in a tree that I had determined to be unclimbable, above a rock covered bluff. The tree I had ridden over to jump onto this tree had sprung back way to far too even consider trying to jump back onto, so there was no possible way to use it to help me get down. I was alone and no one had any idea where I was or when I'd be back. There were no cell phones back then and I had left my gun on the ground, so I had no way to signal for help. I still remember, just like it was yesterday, clinging onto the cracks in the bark of that tree high above the rocky bluff as I inched my way over the huge bulge, thinking at any moment I would fall to my death on the rocks far below me! God must have been with me that night, for I was able to reach the ground without even getting a scratch. There was no way anyone less than an extremely talented rock climber could have done what I had just done. So again, I want to emphasize that a greater power than me had to have been there with me that night. This was another time during my life when God saw me through a life and death situation.

Later when Cindi, our daughter, was small, a friend of ours gave her a Pointer puppy that she named Patches. In those days during the seventies, there were still lots of quail just like when I was younger, so I trained patches to hunt them. My good friend, Kenny Wilson and I hunted quail together for several years during that time. I remember one year during that time that I got over one hundred quail. It wasn't going to last though, as one winter during the late seventies we got a lot of snow and ice and it stayed cold for a long time. Most of the quail in our area didn't survive that winter. The next year Kenny and I hunted hard the first day of the season. We didn't find one single quail where we would have normally found five or six coveys. Ever since then, we've never had very many quail in this area. They still have cycles of good years and bad years, but even in the good years there are very few quail as compared to the way it was before that bad winter. I miss those hunts, but I don't go any more in hopes they will recover to good numbers again.

During the seventies we raised several litters of Pointer pups. One year, I kept two of the female pups that were born on the fourth of July. I named them Lady and Queen. They weren't very old that fall, but I decided to take them for a hunt with their mother, Patches, anyway. To my amazement, they honored and pointed right from the start. After just a few hunts, Lady was as good an all around bird dog as I had ever hunted with. She was a natural at everything she did. I remember once when I shot at a quail watching her go in the direction it flew and not coming back for a long time. I was sure I had missed and was aggravated that she had disappeared. She proved to be smarter than I was, because when she finally showed up she was holding the quail I thought I'd missed in her mouth. Its hard to explain how sometimes you bond with certain animals. It was as if we each knew what the other one was thinking because she usually did what I wanted her to do without any command or signal from me. She was my favorite dog ever, I really loved that little dog.

    Whenever I was around other hunters, I would brag about how good she was and said even though she was only a few months old I'd put her up against anybody's dog of any age. I guess the word got around about how good she was, because before the beginning of the next hunting season she disappeared. I searched everywhere for her and tried everything I could to find her, but not a trace was found and no one had seen her. I always thought someone had heard about how good she was and she was stolen, but I'll never know. I had only had her one hunting season as a pup and then she was gone. There will never be another one to take her place. She was one of a kind, and I still miss her.

Chapter
13

To Run Like the Wind

From the time I was old enough to run, I was always a pretty fast runner. When I wasn't very old, I challenged my Dad to a race to see who was the fastest. I suppose that doesn't seem all that unusual, except that the race was to be me against him on a Ford tractor. Those tractors could run up to fourteen miles an hour, and I was pretty sure I could run faster than that. When we started out, I was in the lead and was sure I was going to win, but there was just one thing wrong with my plan. I started to wear out, and the tractor just kept going the same speed. I hadn't thought about that before I told Dad I could outrun him on that old tractor, I lost!

I learned two lessons that day: Don't be overconfident and to think things through before opening my mouth. I wish I could always remember those two lessons, but unfortunately, sometimes I still don't think about them until it's too late.

In the rural school I attended for six of my eight grade school years, we didn't have an organized sports program. When I started high school, I didn't have experience in any of the sports the school offered. Most of the guys that came out for basketball and baseball had been going to school in town and had been involved in those sports for several years, while those of us from the rural schools had to start from nothing. I really didn't care all that much as I was more interested in hunting, fishing and exploring than school sports at that time anyway.

I still remember being embarrassed in the P.E. class whenever the coach would instruct us to play a game I wasn't familiar with. I had never even dribbled or shot a basketball until I was a freshman in high school, and I had never heard of the game of volleyball. By the time I was good enough to consider trying out for

Chapter 13 - TO RUN LIKE THE WIND

any of the sports I was interested in, the teams were pretty much set.

When I was a senior, the school decided to start a football and track program. Most of the seniors decided not to try out for football, as it was to be a building program and they were only going to play B teams that first year.

However, track seemed like something I would like to try. I was in good physical shape from all the hiking, climbing and running in the bluffs in Rocky Hollow where I had grown up, and I had reached the place where I could outdo almost everyone in my P.E. class. So, I came out for track and liked it right from the start. Our coach thought I would do best in the sprints, and while I was fast, there were a couple of guys a little bit faster. I wanted to try out for the half mile, but our coach said I wasn't built for the half mile as I was too muscular. I finally talked him into letting me try out for it anyway, and then I came down with a soaking bad cold and missed the tryout.

As I watched the group run the half mile tryout that day, I learned a very important lesson. Most of the guys started out running as fast as they could at the start and had to slow down or stop before they reached the finish line. Only a few of them were able to finish with a decent time. So the lesson I learned that day was that it's not always the one who starts out the fastest that wins the race, it's the one who runs the smartest. The lesson I learned watching that race can also be applied to many of the situations we will face during our lives.

Our coach picked the runner with the fastest time in the trial to be our half miler for that track season. Most of the track season was over by the time I got over my cold. My coach said if I still wanted to try out for the half mile, I could. So on that faithful day, it was just the coach's top half miler' me, and one other guy who wanted to try out. I ran in third place for most of the race, letting the others set the pace until there was only about two hundred yards left. I had run up bluffs in Rocky Hollow after wild animals, and this seemed easy compared to that experience. I wasn't even out of breath as I sprinted for the finish line, crossing it in first place. Observers said it was as if the other runners had stopped as I went by them that day.

The next race we were scheduled to compete in was the district meet. I had only run one half mile race in my life, and now I was to be our top half miler at

Chapter 13 - TO RUN LIKE THE WIND

district. Sometimes things have a way of working out and sometimes they don't. I have always thought that this is what kept me from going to the state track meet that year. When I showed up for track two days before our district meet, I found out track had been cancelled as the track coach was attending a meeting somewhere. We were told we could either go to study hall or go to the P.E. class at that time. I liked the P.E. class so I decided to attend it, which turned out to be a big mistake. A student teacher was in charge of the P.E. class that day, and apparently he was trying to prove something as he made us do continuous calisthenics that entire period. I was in good shape and usually enjoyed doing calisthenics, but that day was the most extreme workout any of us had ever gone through. Every muscle in my body was sore by the time the class was over.

So, there I was two days later, stiff and sore on the starting line of the district track meet, with no idea whether I'd be able to run a good race or not. I really had no choice. It was now or never, so I got ready for the starting gun. At the gun, away we went! There was to be no following the leader and sprinting for the finish in this race, as from the very start it was obvious this was to be a fast race. I basically ran the entire race as fast as I could under the circumstances, with nothing left at the finish. My time was two minutes, seven seconds, and I would go to state if I didn't get bumped by someone in the second heat. After all the heats were run, I missed going to state by one place.

Could I have competed at state if I hadn't been stiff and sore from all the calisthenics I had done two days before the meet? How fast could I have been if I would have had a chance to run in track all four years while I was in high school? I'll never know the answers to those questions, but I have wondered about them ever since that day! It was so easy for me to run the half mile when I wasn't stiff and sore that day in the tryouts. I've always felt that with some experience, I would have been running it under two minutes, but I'll never know for sure. The track coach said maybe I should try out for track when I went to college, but college wasn't in my plans, so it appeared my competitive running was over.

I continued to run on my own, off and on for several years, just for the fun of it. Then when I was in my early fifties, I heard about track and field events for

Chapter 13 - TO RUN LIKE THE WIND

seniors over fifty. I liked the thought of being able to run competitively again, but I didn't like the thought of being considered a senior.

In 1996, when I was fifty four years old, I entered the Great River Golden Games in Quincy, Illinois. When I got ready to compete in my first event, the officials pulled me aside and said I couldn't compete in these games as you had to be over fifty years old in order to participate. When I told them I was fifty four, they carded me and that made my day! I came in second or third in several events at several different meets that year, and vowed to train harder so I could do better the next year.

I competed in five or six out of the next ten years, and won at least one first place in every event in my age group, from the four hundred meter dash to the 5K run. So, now am I able to be satisfied in my own mind that I have proven that I am a good runner? I guess the answer to that question is "not quite yet!" So far, my best finish in my age group, in the Hannibal Cannibal 5K, was third place in 2007. If I can get into good enough shape to run it in the future, I'd still like to try to win my age bracket in that race. If I could win it, would I be satisfied then? "Who knows?"

Chapter 14

Those Crazy Teens

As we grow older, we tend to look at the teenagers of today and make remarks such as "look at what those crazy teenagers are doing now!" We tend to forget or we rationalize what we did when we were teenagers. So this isn't about the teenagers of today, but about the teenagers of my time and some of the crazy things I did as a teenager. I'll start with three events where God must have been with me or I might not have survived.

The first of these happened one day when some of my friends and I decided we wanted to explore the area on the other side of South River. We had explored almost everything on the north side, and like most adventurers, wanted to see some new territory.

We set out early that morning in order to have a full day of exploration into the unknown. It was during the latter part of the winter, and as we approached the river, we were concerned about whether we would be able to cross on the ice or not. There had been several deep snows earlier in the winter, and the rivers in the area were beginning to rise. The temperatures during the past few days had gradually been getting warmer and we were afraid the ice might have broken up on the river, making it impossible for us to cross. This was our first opportunity of that year for a new adventure, so we trudged on, hoping for the best. When we finally got to the river, we were pleasantly surprised to find a place where we could still cross on the frozen ice without a problem.

We spent most of the day exploring the bluffs and canyons on that side of the river. The sound of a distant train, carried there by the south wind, was our only connection to the outside world. The weather warmed up that afternoon so much that most of the snow was melting. It created waterfalls as it rushed down the rocky streams toward the river. We

Chapter 14 - THOSE CRAZY TEENS

An Ice Jam similar to the one mentioned in this story. Picture courtesy of NOAA 2007

were enjoying ourselves so much we hadn't realized how late in the day it was becoming.

When we finally headed back to cross the river, we knew we would have to hurry or we'd never make it before dark. We didn't anticipate any problem crossing back to the other side. We should have known that with all that snow melting, the river would be running much higher. When we arrived at the river, we saw that the ice had broken up into huge slabs. Some of them were as much as a foot thick and eight or ten feet across.

It was a four mile round trip to the nearest bridge, and it was going to be dark soon, so we started looking for a place where we might be able to cross. We found an ice jam where the ice had piled up and decided to cross there. I waited, and was the last one to cross it. About the time I was half way across, the entire ice jam started shifting under my feet. I barely made it to the other side before the whole thing gave way and surged down the river! I was a good swimmer, but I wouldn't have had a chance in that ice jam.

The other two both involved too much speed, for some reason like most teenagers, during that time of my life I liked to drive fast. One night, I was driving my parents '57 Chevrolet on a gravel road I wasn't familiar with, and as usual I was going entirely too fast. I came over a steep hill and saw a very narrow iron rail bridge at the bottom of it. I was going too fast to be sure I'd get across it, so I hit my brakes. When I did the loose gravel on that hill put me into a skid. The car turned completely sideways as it slid towards that bridge. In desperation, I was trying to steer out of that skid, but it appeared I was going to hit those iron rails broadside! At the very last second, the car straightened out and I crossed the bridge without a scratch. It had all happened in seconds, but in my mind it had seemed as though I had been sliding

Chapter 14 - THOSE CRAZY TEENS

towards that bridge for a long time and it left me exhausted.

While I was still in high school, I bought a Harley Davidson model 74 motorcycle. I'm not sure how I got my parents to agree to let me buy "that thing," as my aunt who didn't approve of motorcycles called it. It was a big thing, and was the most powerful one they made at that time. I had made enough money to pay for it, so maybe that had something to do with them letting me buy it.

A buddy of mine had a Harley Sportster, which was a size smaller, but just as fast. He was always bugging me to race, but me being the more level headed one, usually said no. Then one night on a blacktop near our homes, he gave me a sign that was a challenge to race him, and away he went speeding down the road. For some reason I threw caution to the wind that night and the race was on! He later told me that as I passed him that night, fire was shooting out of the twin pipes on my 74 at least ten feet behind me.

The blacktop was hilly just ahead of us, and we should have slowed down, but we didn't. At the top of each hill, our motorcycles were both leaving the ground as we went flying over those hills. When I glanced down at my speedometer, it said one hundred twenty five miles per hour! How we kept from wrecking those things, I'll never know, and we didn't even wear helmets back then. I don't imagine they would have helped at those speeds even if we would have been wearing them. On one of the hills, when my buddy's bike left the ground his engine blew, which was a blessing in disguise for that ended the race.

So, looking back over the years, have I been just plain lucky, or was God with me when I did these crazy things, as well as other situations I tell about in this book? I believe God has a plan for me and he was with me and will be with me until I have done everything he put me on this earth to do.

I had several other close calls on my Harley before I finally traded it for a car, so maybe I was supposed to start dating this particular girl when I was a senior in high school. I can't remember if she didn't like motorcycles, or if it was because her parents wouldn't let her ride on mine with me. I traded my motorcycle for a 1955 Ford car. It was nothing fancy, but it was mine. I've been told that if I would have kept that Harley, it would be worth ten

Chapter 14 - THOSE CRAZY TEENS

thousand dollars or more now. I'm sure that old car has been junked a long time ago. I guess that's just the way it works out sometimes. As the saying goes, "no use crying over spilt milk."

Anyway back to that girl, one night she wanted me to teach her how to drive. We were on a country gravel road with no traffic, late at night, so I decided to let her drive. "Big mistake!" She hadn't gone a mile when she ran over a mailbox. When we got out and looked at it, we saw that the box itself was only slightly dented, but the post it was mounted on was completely out of the ground. I took her home, got a shovel, and went back in the middle of the night and reset the mailbox. We were never sure if anyone suspected it had happened or not.

During the summers, my friends and I spent a lot of time swimming in the rivers. Our favorite place to swim was at Horseshoe Bend on North River. There was a deep swimming hole just below the old iron truss bridge that crossed the river there. We tied a rope on a tree limb that hung out over the water where it was around twelve feet deep at that time. We would take the rope and climb as high on the side of the bluff as the length of the rope would let us, and swing out over the

Iron Truss Bridge

water where we'd drop in from around ten feet in the air.

Some of us guys decided just dropping straight down was getting old, so we started trying different things. I can't take credit for the flip dive one of the guys came up with that day, but we all learned to do it. We would swing as high as possible, do a flip in the air, and dive head first into the deepest part of the water. Kids our ages came from all over to swim there, so those of us that could do the flip dive had a blast showing off for them. It was almost as much fun watching them try to learn that dive as it was doing it. We got to see them do belly flops, back flops and hit the water in every position imaginable. Some of them got good at it, but a lot more of them never did get to where they could do it at all. It wasn't all fun, as occasionally someone would get injured. I wasn't there when it happened, but I know one guy got a broken arm when he didn't let go of the rope, swung back, and hit the tree.

After a long winter when it first got warm enough for us to go swimming again, we headed there for our first swim of the year. I grabbed the rope and climbed as high as I could get in order to swing out as far and high as possible. I made a perfect flip and dove head first into the water that was less than waste deep, hitting my head on the sandbar that had filled in part of our swimming hole. The pain shot through my neck and into my back like a lightning bolt! There were several kids swimming there that day, but none of them said anything about how the water was a lot shallower than it had been the year before when they saw me getting ready to dive. Of course, one of us should have checked the depth before we began to dive, but it had always been deep there and on the surface, it looked the same. That was the last flip dive I ever did there, as after every big rain, our favorite swimming

Our favorite swimming hole at Horseshoe Bend

hole kept getting shallower. It wasn't long before we quit going there at all. I guess that old swimming hole was the thing that had held my group of friends together, because for the most part we pretty much went our separate ways after that.

Everything has changed there now. The old iron bridge has been replaced with a new concrete bridge and the swimming hole has continued to fill in. The tree where we tied the rope died, and was washed away long ago. The people who own the property on the side where we climbed as high as we could to swing off the rope, have now put up a locked gate with a no trespassing sign on it.

The Conservation Commission bought the land on the other side of the river and renamed the area Horseshoe Bluff because they already had an area named Horseshoe Bend.

Whenever I drive by there, I remember how it was back when we were teenagers. Occasionally, it's as if I'm there again, making that perfect flip dive off that rope into that cool water below me. At other times, I here the laughter as we watch someone new try to do it.

Those days and the things we did when I was growing up were gone long ago, but I hope somehow, writing about them will make the memories of them last forever.

Chapter
15

The Timely Breakdown

In the year 2000, a new bridge was opened to cross the Mississippi River from Hannibal, Missouri into Illinois. At that same location, many years earlier during the 1970's , I had another one of those close calls that have occurred throughout my life. I was hauling corn in my two ton truck to the Bunge Elevator in East Hannibal without a thought of how close to a possible fatal accident I had come that day. At that time, Highway 36 that crossed the old Mark Twain Memorial Bridge was still two lanes.
As you approached the bridge from the west, you went down a long hill. It was necessary to apply your brakes several times to keep from gaining too much

speed, as there was a curve just before you entered the bridge and the bridge, was also very narrow.

One day as I drove down the hill towards the bridge, I remember how the heavy load of corn seemed to be pushing my truck to go faster. I had to apply the brakes almost continually to keep my speed under control and was able to cross the bridge without incident.

There was a long line at the elevator that day, and I had to wait over an hour before unloading my truck. Finally, I was on my way back to the field, where I was sure there would be another load ready for me to haul. I'm not sure how fast I was driving that day, but I'm sure it was too fast.

Thankfully, the road by the field was long and flat, for when I applied the brakes they hit the floor. I had absolutely no brakes at all! The lever on my emergency brake had broken off and hadn't worked in over a year, so it was of no use either. All I could do was downshift through the gears as my speed gradually decreased. Eventually, to my relief, I came to a stop about a half mile down the road from where I had first hit my brakes. When I checked the brake fluid reservoir, I discovered it was totally empty. A rock or something had knocked a small hole in one of the brake lines, and the fluid had all leaked out.

Then it hit me! If I had lost my brakes going down that hill toward the bridge with that heavy load of corn, I wouldn't have had any way of controlling my speed. I would have either crashed into that bridge, or would have been forced to purposely crash into something before I reached the bridge in order to stop the truck. So was I just lucky that day or was God watching over me again? By now you should know what I believe!

Chapter
16

The Lure of the Canyon

It was August of 1960, the year I graduated from high school, when our family decided to go for a long trip out

Grand Canyon south Rim View

west. When we were ready to leave home, we had trouble finding keys to lock all the doors. You see, most people who lived on the farms back then never locked their homes unless they were going to be gone for several days. After a long delay, we finally found the keys and we were on our way.

I can't remember very much about our trip until we reached the south rim of the Grand Canyon in Arizona. When we walked out on a lookout point for our first view into the Canyon, we were in awe! There isn't a way to describe it in a way that anyone would be prepared for how they feel when they first see it. Everyone just stands there in silence, as it seems to leave them all speechless.

We spent most of the morning taking in the views, and then went into the trading post to get a few mementoes of our trip. I met a Park Ranger who told me that there were trails that led to the bottom of the Canyon. He also said that if you booked in advance, you could stay at a place called Phantom Ranch, where there was a main lodge and cabins.

I was told there was two ways to get to the Phantom Ranch. You either went by mule train or walked. The ranger said the mule trains were already on their way to the bottom for the day, and I would have needed a reservation anyway. When I told him that I would just walk down, he started giving me all the reasons why I shouldn't even consider doing such a foolish thing. He said everyone starts down early in the morning in order to reach the bottom before the middle of the afternoon, which is the hottest part of the day. It was almost noon, I wasn't prepared to start the hike, and he reminded me again that I wouldn't have a place to stay when I got there. I had already told him I didn't bring any camping equipment, so he knew that wasn't an option.

 When I kept insisting, he finally gave me the phone number of the Phantom Ranch, thinking when I found out there wasn't any place for me to stay I'd give up. I had to call from a pay phone in order to reach the Phantom Ranch, where they said they had a cancellation and had one cabin available. When I said I'd take it, they advised me not to try to walk down during the heat of the day, just as the Park Ranger had told me earlier.

 I think I convinced them I'd be able to take the heat by telling them I'd been bucking bales of hay in the heat for most of the summer, back in Missouri. Upon hearing that, they reluctantly agreed to let me attempt the 9.8 mile hike down the Bright Angel Trail to the Phantom Ranch. I didn't tell them I had absolutely no hiking gear with me at all. I didn't even actually have real hiking boots. I had a pair of logger boots that were rugged enough, but they were heavy and the heels were fairly thick. So that was what I wore, as that was my only choice. I didn't have anything to carry water in, so Mom gave me a quart plastic jar of water, and I was ready to go.

When I finally started down the trail, it was one o-clock in the afternoon. Time-wise and equipment-wise, I was probably about as ill prepared as anyone could be when I started out. The thing I had going for me however, was that I was in excellent shape and I was eighteen years old!

Once I got away from the crowds along the rim, I had the trail to myself. Everyone else had already retreated from the heat of the afternoon. The deeper I hiked into the Canyon, the hotter it became, but it didn't seem to bother me. I was enjoying the views and the hike too much to worry about the heat.

The trail was narrow, steep and was all downhill. In places, there were sheer

Chapter 16 - THE LURE OF THE CANYON

drop- offs of several hundred feet. I wondered if anyone ever fell to their death from the narrow trail as I continued on my way.

Down close to the bottom of the canyon, I met a young couple who were hiking out. They seemed to be just as surprised as I was that anyone would be hiking in the extreme heat. When they asked me about the plastic jar that I was carrying for my only water supply, I acted as if it was some new high tech water bottle. I wondered if they saw right through my ploy. We visited a few minutes and then continued on our journeys. It was obvious they were in excellent condition and would have no trouble hiking out in the heat of the day.

When I reached the Colorado River, I knew I only had a little over a mile and a half left until I reached the Phantom Ranch. In order to make sure my water lasted I had saved almost half of it, so I took another good drink.

Before long, I came to the Bright Angel Suspension Bridge that spanned the river. It was just wide enough for the mule trains to cross and was high above the river. When I reached the other side, I decided to go down to the edge of the river. I had been told that the evening meal would be served around eight and it was still early, so I knew I had plenty of time to do a little exploring. When I reached the edge of the river, it was obvious that the current was extremely strong, and anyone foolish enough to get in it would be swept away with very little hope of survival. This was before the time that the Glen Canyon Dam had been built, and the river still ran wild and free.

I had never heard a rattlesnake before, but when one rattled in the rocks a few feet in front of me, there was no doubt as to what it was. My desire to go any further in that direction was definitely over, and I headed back to the trail.

It only took me a few more minutes to reach the Phantom Ranch. It was among a few scattered trees that grew along the spring fed Bright Angel Creek. When I signed in for the night, I could tell they were surprised I had arrived so early. They said as hot as it was that day, they had wondered if I'd be able to get there at all. Back at that time, there was a swimming pool there, and luckily they had a few pairs of swimming trunks for sale, so I got to go for a refreshing swim before our dinner was served.

The dinner was served ranch style at a huge, old wooden table, and the food was

Chapter 16 - THE LURE OF THE CANYON

excellent. While we ate our meal, everyone introduced themselves and told where they were from. I hadn't expected that there would be people there from all over the world. As near as I can remember, there was just a small group of around fifteen people there that night. Some had come by the mule train and others had hiked in, leaving before daylight in order to get there before the heat of the day. When it was my turn to tell about myself, some of the other guests couldn't believe I had left the south rim at one o-clock in the afternoon. I was told of people that had to be rescued because of heat stroke on a fairly regular basis during the summer. We visited for some time after the meal, and some of the stories of the more experienced hikers were amazing.

When we all decided to retire for the night, the ones that were hiking out early the next morning were given a sack of food to take with them. I was surprised at how modern the cabins were. They even had air conditioning, which was a good thing, as it was still hot outside. I wondered how they got all the materials down there to build the cabins and furnish them, as there was absolutely no way to drive anything close to that area. I set the alarm for four o-clock a.m. in order to get an early start for my hike all uphill back to the south rim. I knew it was going to be more strenuous hiking back out.

The next thing I remember was the alarm going off, and me wishing I had gone to bed earlier. I got up and headed out just as it was getting light. Even though it was cooler than it had been when I went to bed, I'm sure it still must have been around ninety degrees. As I looked at the Phantom Ranch, I wondered if I'd ever see it again. I crossed back over the suspension bridge, followed the trail along the river, and started the long climb back to the south rim. Up ahead of me I could see the father and his two sons I'd met the night before already on the switchbacks some distance away. I decided I'd try to catch up with them if I could.

I hadn't noticed the weight of those logger boots on the way down, but on the way up, they felt like they weighed ten pounds each! This was definitely going to be a more strenuous hike than the one on the way in. I came to a place where a phone line cut across the country to the Phantom Ranch. (I don't think it's there anymore). I thought it must be a shorter way back to the south rim and decided to follow it. Looking back now, I know I shouldn't have done that, but keep in mind I was eighteen then. My reasoning, at the time, was that if they were able to put in that line, then I'd be able to follow it, so I did. It was pretty rugged in places, and I began to wonder where I might come out.

I was really beginning to feel that I had made a very bad decision and started wondering what I should do next. Finally, to my great relief, I caught sight of the trail up ahead. When I got back on the trail, I looked ahead of me for the father and his two sons, but they weren't there. When I looked back down the trail, there they were about the same distance behind me as they had been in front of me before. So unless they had stopped to rest, I must have cut around a mile off the trip back to the south rim. Regardless of whether I did or not, I realize looking back, it was a risky move to make!

When I finally reached the south rim, Dad, Mom, and my sister Beth were waiting there relieved, and ready to continue the rest of our trip. Even though I was in good shape, I was pretty worn out. After getting something to eat, I was ready to lie in the back seat and take a long nap! It had been quite an adventure, and it wasn't long before I was planning to return to walk the canyon rim to rim. I had no idea, at the time, that it would be forty-one years before I would get the chance to actually walk from the south rim to the north rim, but that's another story!

Chapter
17

Rescue in the Grand Canyon

"That lady is in trouble!" I told Paul as we entered the top of Devil's Corkscrew on the Bright Angel Trail in Grand Canyon, Arizona. Just then, she stumbled and fell, rolling toward a drop of several hundred feet.

Little did we know when we started planning our backpacking trip what lay before us. For me, it all began back in 1960, when at age eighteen, I had walked from the south rim of the Grand Canyon down the Bright Angel Trail 9.8 miles to Phantom Ranch. After spending the night there, I returned to the south rim on the same trail the next morning. Ever since, I had hoped to return and walk the Canyon rim to rim.

Paul Osborne, my son-in law, and I started planning the backpacking trip in May, when we received our back-country permits for a four day trip from the south rim to the north rim. We then started increasing our conditioning routine. My routine included riding a bike up to ten miles a day, walking with a forty-five pound backpack up to seven miles a day, in addition to weight lifting. Paul was also biking long distances and carrying his weighted pack.

My wife Connie, Cindi our daughter, Paul and I left Kansas City on Saturday, September 1, 2001 for the Grand Canyon area. We arrived in Sedona, Arizona on Sunday, where we planned to take in a

Paul, Cindi, Connie and Tom on the South Rim of the Grand Canyon

Chapter 17 - RESCUE IN THE GRAND CANYON

few sights before driving on to the Grand Canyon. Monday had gone as planned with all of us enjoying the breathtaking views of the area. Connie and Cindi had planned to sight-see in Flagstaff and Sedona, while Paul and I hiked the canyon. The plan was for them to meet us at the north rim on the fourth day as we walked out.

On Tuesday, the four of us walked from our lodge near the Canyon rim to the head of the Bright Angel Trail. Before starting out, we took pictures and I dedicated our walk to my parents who had both passed away since our family trip to the area in 1960. We then said our good-byes, and Paul and I started off on what was to become a much greater adventure than any of us could imagine at the time.

It wasn't long before I was wishing I had trimmed a few more pounds from the forty-five pound pack I was carrying, since my knees were taking a beating on the steep downhill slope. We stopped for breaks at the 1.5 and 3 mile water stations, and again at Indian Garden, about 4.6 miles down. In spite of my sore knees, we were enjoying the spectacular views and pausing occasionally to take pictures.

As we continued, the trail crossed a stream and followed an inner canyon for some distance before crossing a hogback-a high ridge with steeply sloping sides. We then descended into a part of the canyon aptly named Devil's Corkscrew, where we witnessed a lady falling and rolling toward the edge of the steep cliff! Paul, who was ahead of me on the trail, was able to grab her just before she rolled off the edge. He then helped her to sit down on the trail, where it seemed she would be safe. While he was taking off his pack, she managed to stand and started stumbling backwards towards the edge again. One more step and she would fallen over the edge! This time, I grabbed her just before she fell to a certain death. She appeared to weigh approximately two hundred pounds, and it took every bit of strength I had to keep her from falling over the edge. I then managed to drag her over against the wall, where she was now unable to even sit up without help. Meanwhile, her husband, who had been unable to help with the situation, was obviously not doing very well either.

It had become obvious that we had to get the couple to a safer place back up the trail, so Paul and I left our packs

Chapter 17 - RESCUE IN THE GRAND CANYON

against the rock wall to be retrieved later. As Paul shouldered her backpack, I got the woman to her feet and we started backtracking. She had virtually no muscle control, and I was having difficulty gaining much distance until Paul held her by the other arm as we struggled slowly up the steep trail. We learned that she had several medical conditions and was also taking a number of different medications.

As luck would have it, after about two hundred yards of this, we met a mule train coming down the trail. The wrangler in the lead quickly saw our situation and got off his mule to assist us. We told him the woman would never make it without help and passed on the information about her medical conditions. At that point, the wrangler called the park rangers to send a helicopter to fly her out. We agreed to get her back to the creek we had crossed earlier where she could rest and cool off. The mule train continued on and after a great deal of effort, we finally managed to arrive at the creek,where we waited for the helicopter to arrive.

Our plan for arriving at the Bright Angel Campground before the extreme heat of the day set in had been drastically changed at this point. We hadn't hiked even half the distance and the heat was already getting intense. Paul and I were also worried about the amount of energy we had used up. Our problem was that we hated to leave them in such bad condition, so we decided to wait a while longer.

The condition of the woman and her husband seemed to have improved somewhat after cooling off in the spring-fed creek, so after a long delay, we decided we had no choice but to go on since our water and food were back where we had left our packs. We also knew the wrangler had given the rangers a detailed description of where the couple would be and figured it would be only a matter of time before the helicopter would fly them out, so we left the couple there to wait and headed back down the canyon towards our packs. As we walked back across the hogback, we remembered the condors that Paul had been hoping to see during the trip. The mule train wrangler had pointed some out to his group, but they were no longer in the area.

When we got to our packs, we discovered that they were in direct sunlight against the rock wall and our water, Gatorade, and food were extremely hot. We knew the warmer our liquids

Chapter 17 - RESCUE IN THE GRAND CANYON

were, the slower they would be absorbed into our systems. Unfortunately, there were no more water stations the rest of the way to our camp, which was still several miles away. We choked down a small amount of the hot liquids and decided to go on down the trail before looking for a shady place to eat.

At that moment, we heard the rescue helicopter. It made a few circles of the area, but it looked as though they might not be able to spot the couple along the creek. We immediately started back up the trail, signaling their location to the pilot. He landed along the side of the trail and when one of the rangers approached us, we told him everything about the

Paul and Me by Helicopter

situation. He told us we could go on and they would fly the couple out to the hospital. We were so relieved that help had arrived that we paused long enough to take a few pictures by the helicopter.

The next big challenge we faced was hiking through the hottest part of the canyon during the hottest part of the day. We knew that hikers were warned against attempting this, but we decided to continue on without realizing how much of our energy reserves we had burned up. Our situation was also complicated by the fact that our food and drinks were so hot.

Our pace was much slower after that, since we knew we had to conserve our energy in order to get to the campground. As we moved along the trail, we discussed the events of the day and realized that a power much greater than ours was involved in saving the woman and her husband. If we had been only a few seconds later, it would have been too late. It had to be God's plan for us to be in that exact spot on the trail at that exact moment. It was such a powerful feeling, that even as I write this today, it still brings tears to my eyes.

Finally, we found a shady place along Devil's Corkscrew to try to eat a very late lunch. We knew we needed the

Chapter 17 - RESCUE IN THE GRAND CANYON

energy, but both the temperature and our supplies were so hot, we were only able to choke down a small amount. We watched as the rescue helicopter took off in the distance and were relieved to know for sure that the couple had gotten out of the canyon.

One of the three rangers on the rescue team, who had not flown out with the couple, later passed us on the trail. He inquired about our condition and we assured him that we were tough and would be fine. During the rescue I had completely forgotten about the pain in my knees, but now they were hurting much worse than before. I decided not to let the ranger know how bad they were hurting, even though the pain was becoming almost unbearable.

By this time, the trail, which had been filled with people from all over the world near the rim earlier in the day, was virtually empty. Most of the hikers and backpackers that had ventured deep into the canyon had already reached their destinations before the afternoons intense heat had arrived, but we still had several miles to go before reaching the campground. We finally reached the Colorado River and were amazed when we realized we had to climb back up to the

Bright Angel suspension bridge 1.5 miles up the river.

After taking some Advil, my knees finally stopped hurting and I increased the pace while going up the slope. Paul, however, was now the one needing frequent rest stops. After one particular long break, I began to have leg cramps when I got up. We had been perspiring heavily for several hours and knew we should have eaten more salty food earlier in the day, and now the Gatorade and trail mixes weren't able bring our sodium levels back up. The conversation and laughter that we had kept up during most of the day was dwindling down to the point where very little was being said, as we struggled to complete the final leg of our journey for that day. When the bridge appeared around a bend about a fourth of a mile ahead, I knew we were going to make it. Even so, it took us another half hour to reach it, because we were both hurting so badly at that point.

We finally reached the Bright Angel Campground around five PM, three or four hours later than our original plan. The thermometer, which they keep in the sun to convince hikers not to hike in the heat of the day, still read 112 degrees, but we had made it! While Paul collapsed on the table by our campsite, I went to fill up our water supplies.

Along the way, I met the ranger who had passed us on the trail. He was telling another ranger the details of our rescue mission and dubbed us "the heroes of the day."

While Paul prepared our freeze-dried meals, I decided to cool off in Bright Angel Creek. When I got into the icy cold, spring-fed creek, my legs and hands immediately started cramping. The cramps were so severe, I wasn't sure if I would be able to get back up the thirty-foot slope. By the time I managed to get there, Paul had our meals ready, however, I was unable to eat mine because it was making me feel nauseated. I couldn't believe it! I hadn't been sick to my stomach over two or three times in the last ten years, but this stuff just wasn't going to stay down!

We had learned that the Gatorade we had been drinking was not sufficient to replace our salt under such extreme conditions, While Paul asked at some other campsites for some salt to replenish our bodies, I started feeling really sick. At that point, the thought crossed my mind that I might not be able to continue to the north rim. Even though we never discussed the possibility, I wondered if Paul wasn't thinking the same thing. This trip had been a goal of mine for a long time, and I resolved right then that a few hardships were not going to keep me from achieving it. Nobody was going to fly me out of this canyon!

Paul soon returned with some runners gel and salt. After eating some of the gel and drinking some salted water, the cramps and nausea began to subside, and Paul and I were able to sleep through the night.

Although we were both very sore the next morning, we felt amazingly well considering what we had been through the previous day. The freeze-dried breakfast tasted good, and we were both optimistic that we would continue to feel better as we enjoyed the day around Phantom Ranch and at our campsite. After lunch, we walked two miles on nearby trails to try to loosen up our muscles, but as soon as we stopped walking, they would tighten up again. We were questioning whether we would be ready to hike the 14.2 miles plus side trips, as we headed for the north rim for the next two days.

We attended a program presented at the Phantom Ranch and were amazed

Chapter 17 - RESCUE IN THE GRAND CANYON 133

to learn that the youngest rocks in the canyon were older than the dinosaurs. We also learned that the U. S. had a transcontinental railroad before the canyon was ever explored. That evening, while eating a family-style supper, we had a chance to share experiences with several of the other hikers from all over the world.

When we woke up the next morning, we were pleasantly surprised that all our soreness was gone. We broke camp and ate a good breakfast before heading up the North Kaibab Trail. About a mile from Cottonwood Campground, we crossed a swiftly running creek and headed up a steep trail to Ribbon Falls, which was a beautiful, isolated place. We walked up behind the falls and stood on a sixty-foot tall rock underneath it. As we were standing there, the wind shifted and we were drenched in ice cold spring water from the falls. Even though it soaked us and filled our boots, it felt great! It was such a wonderful place that we spent two hours there before heading on to Cottonwood Campground, where the thermometer, again placed in the sun, read 117 degrees!

After eating, we decided to go to the creek to cool off. When Paul put his feet in, he swore the water was 33 degrees and said there was no way he was getting in it. I was really feeling good and decided to show him up, so I actually swam in it. Paul said he always suspected that I was crazy, and now he knew that I was for sure. He was joking, I think!

That evening, we heard from other hikers and a park employee that the most difficult part of our hike still lay ahead of us. We didn't think it could possibly be any harder than our first day! It got as cold that night as it had been hot that day, but we slept well and woke up refreshed and ready to go.

We headed for the north rim at 6:50 AM, and soon were in an area that I considered to be the most beautiful of the entire trip. As we climbed higher, each view was more spectacular than the last. We passed Roaring Falls, which had a much larger flow than Ribbon Falls. It gushed out of the side of a cliff and cascaded down to the creek below. The overlooks and vertical drops continued to be higher. Some almost took your breath away! In places, the trail would narrow to as little as three or four feet wide, with a rock wall straight up on one side and a vertical drop of a thousand feet or more on the other side. The elevation had been

4080 feet at the Cottonwood Campground and was 8250 feet at the north rim trailhead, which meant we were hiking over 4000 feet in elevation in a single day! Just imagine the steepest slope you could climb without sliding backwards, and that would describe what much of this trail was like.

Two miles from the north rim, we stopped to cook a meal and rest before our final leg of the trip. It was an emotional time for me. I had looked forward to crossing the canyon for so long and was about to reach that goal, but the canyon had gotten into my blood and I hated to leave it. As we climbed higher, we agreed that even though this section of the trail was very strenuous, it didn't compare with our stress filled, exhausting first day.

As we approached the north rim, we looked across the Grand Canyon to the south and could see Mount Humphrey, the tallest mountain in Arizona, some sixty miles away. What a spectacular view! At that point, we had reached the pine forest located along the north rim so we knew we were getting close to the end of our journey.

We were taking a few last pictures before leaving the canyon, when we looked up to see Cindi coming down the trail toward us, She walked the rest of the way out to the north rim with us, where Connie was waiting. What started out to be a crossing from rim to rim had turned into an adventure of a lifetime, and the memories of it will last forever!

Chapter
18

Our Changing World

Exactly one hundred years ago both of my parents were born in the year 1912. If they were alive today, they would be amazed at how much our world has changed in the last few years since they passed from this earth. As I write this today in 2012, a whole century of time and changes have taken place since their birth. Some of the changes have been for the good and some have not. Even from the time when I was a small boy during the 1940's to the present time, there have been many changes.

As we journey back in time throughout the last century, we can easily see many of the changes that have taken place. We will compare how things were back then to the present time in the homes, and on the farms, in the rural areas of northeast Missouri and the surrounding states of the Midwest.

From the outside, the homes today vary, from the newest modern styles to some that were built as long as one hundred years ago. Outside appearances can be deceiving though, for when you enter them, most will have modern conveniences no one even dreamed about years ago.

Most of the homes in the rural areas didn't have electricity until the mid 1940's (after WWII.) Their only lighting was from coal oil lamps and candles. There were no televisions, radios, computers or any of the other things we take for granted today that electricity provides.

Back then, most homes had a cistern or deep well outside the house with a hand pump to draw their water. It had to be carried inside by hand for washing, cooking and drinking. The only way to have hot water was to heat it on a wood cook stove. The stove probably already had a fire in it, as that was the only way people had of cooking their meals, regardless of the weather outside. Even though it was hard work compared to today's standards, cooking and heating their water in the winter wasn't too bad as the heat was needed. If you can, just imagine how hot it got in the summer in those homes!

Today, most homes in the rural areas have hot and cold running water. It's piped in through pipelines from large lakes or rivers, purified and ready to use. The old wood cook stoves have been replaced with modern electric or gas cook tops and ovens. Food can also be heated in seconds or minutes in microwave ovens.

In order to keep food from spoiling in the past, it either had to be canned or cured in some manner. It could be kept in an ice box for a short period of time if you kept a large block of ice in it. Most ice boxes were wood on the outside and metal on the inside, where you kept the food cold with huge blocks of ice. During the winter, if they were lucky and it didn't get too warm outside, some people were able to keep uncured meat frozen in a shed, such as a smokehouse. The smokehouses were used to smoke meat, cure hams, hang cured hams, store lard and many other things. Today's homes have electric refrigerators for keeping food cold. They also have electric freezers where food can be kept frozen for several months until needed. A few people still can fruit or vegetables, but most just don't have the time anymore.

Most people who lived on farms had never heard of an inside bathroom until the middle of the last century. If you needed to use the bathroom, you had to leave the comforts of your home and go out back to an outhouse. It didn't make any difference how bad the weather was, as that was the only option people had. Baths were taken in a galvanized tub, with water heated on the stove. Today's homes have one or more inside bathrooms with tubs, showers, stools, lavatories, cabinets, and mirrors.

The old wood heating stoves have mostly been replaced with central heating and air conditioning systems. In recent years, a few people have gone back to using wood heat because of poor economic conditions, however.

I was told by my grandparents that the farms in our area were mostly from eighty to one hundred sixty acres around the time my parents were born. The land at that time was farmed using horses and small horse drawn equipment. Everything that couldn't be done using horses had to be done by hand. This made it almost impossible for one person to farm any

Chapter 18 - OUR CHANGING WORLD

more acres than that. For some of the big jobs such as haying, woodcutting, and butchering neighbors gathered together on each farm to do the work.

When farm tractors and tractor drawn equipment started showing up on farms, everything started to change. One person could now do the work it had taken several to do in the past. As a result, he could now farm more land. This started a trend that has continued right up until the present time. Tractors and other equipment have continued to get larger and more expensive. Most of the small farms have been bought and combined with others over the years by farmers who want to make more efficient use of their equipment. Now some of the larger farms in our neighborhood consist of several thousand acres.

The original land we now call the Home Place was purchased by my paternal grandparents in 1904. It consisted of one hundred and five acres. They also owned another one hundred and twenty acres now referred to as the Other Place. My Dad added two more parcels of land during his lifetime. He told me he paid a little over thirty dollars an acre for the north fifty acres on our Home Place around 1950. Then in 1960, he bought the sixty-seven acre Scrace Place (named for the former owners) east of the Home Place and paid sixty-five hundred dollars for it. That figures out to only ninety-seven dollars an acre, and both of those farms are highly tillable.

Farmers continue to want to expand their operations. Prices for grain and livestock have been good for the last several years, and land prices have skyrocketed. Land similar to the farms Dad bought, that I mentioned above, is selling for three to five thousand dollars an acre. I've even heard of some land in the Midwest selling for as much as ten thousand dollars an acre.

The 1970's were similar, economy wise, to what they are today on the farm. Farmers were paying what were then record prices for land. Then, along came the 1980's. There were three major droughts in the Midwest during that decade, and yields were terrible. To make matters even worse, interest rates went up to record high levels. Farmers who had gone into debt to buy land and equipment were in trouble. Some of the ones with the most debt went bankrupt, while others were just barely able to hang on.

Chapter 18 - OUR CHANGING WORLD

Most farm wives in the past hadn't worked away from the farm before that time. They had kept busy raising a family, canning, cooking, cleaning, washing, gardening, and doing many other jobs around the farm. However, in order to help hang onto their farms during the 1980's, a large number of farm wives went to work in the surrounding towns. Many of them continue to work at those jobs at the present time.

Modes of transportation have changed substantially over the last one hundred years. The horse and buggy have been replaced with the modern automobile. People now travel greater distances to do their shopping. Also, because of the increased size of the farms, fewer people live in the rural areas. As a result, most of the country stores and some of the stores in smaller towns have had to close. All the country schools have closed, and students are bussed long distances to town. The congregations of many small country churches dwindled down to where many of them had to close their doors for the last time. Some may say all these things are just progress, but I wonder if our rural communities haven't lost a part of what made them a great place to live to begin with!

Over the last one hundred years, some species of wildlife have flourished while others have suffered huge declines. About sixty years ago when Dad and I went out to do our chores, we got a surprise. There, among the sheep, was a whitetail deer. It was the first one I had ever seen in the wild. During the late 1800's, the deer had been hunted down in the Midwest to the point where most areas didn't have any. I've heard that the Missouri Conservation Commission started restocking deer about thirty miles south of us along the Salt River in the 1940's. It's possible that the one we saw came from that area. Now the Conservation Commission estimates there are as many as thirty deer to the square mile in some areas of Missouri.

There were no wild turkeys here until the Conservation Commission reintroduced them several years ago. They have also done very well over the last several years. We used to have, on the average, around ten coveys of quail on our farm. Now, some years I see two coveys, and other years I only see one. When I was growing up, some of our bigger ponds had so many bullfrogs in them that I was unable to count them.

Chapter 18 - OUR CHANGING WORLD

They have suffered a huge decline and I seldom see one anymore.

These are some of the changes that have been most apparent to me in the century since my parents were born. There have been many other changes in the rural areas of the Midwest that I haven't covered here. As I wrote in the beginning of this chapter, some changes have been for the good, and some have not. You be the judge.

Chapter 19

Reflections

Each spring as the days grow longer and the rays of the sun begin to warm the earth, I am again drawn to wander the woods and bluffs of my youth. I have wandered these hills and woods every year since I was a very small boy. They draw me like a magnet.

On this day as I walk through the woods, I am aware of the first signs of spring. The trees are beginning to show a faint hue of green and the redbud trees are in full bloom. Small wildflowers now grow on the south slopes more exposed to the sun. The water from the recently thawed snows flows clear and cold in the streams, as it does each year at this time. The sound of it is music to my ears as it rushes over small waterfalls created by rock ledges in its path. I hear the sound of a flock of geese on their annual flight back to the north, and in some unexplained way this makes me sad. I think it must have something to do with the realization of the passing of time. Time passes so quickly, the days and weeks turn into months and years, and I look back and wonder where it all went! The birds and squirrels sing and chatter with sounds of joy at the prospect of a new spring season and this brings me out of my sad mood.

    As I cross the back fifty acres of our Home Place, I suddenly realize that I am in the area of the giant cottonwood tree where Dad and I saw all those squirrels when I was a small boy. It seems as if it were only yesterday when we were standing there, looking up and trying to count how many were in that tree. I can still hear the reports of Dad's old twelve gauge shotgun ringing in my ears, even though I realize it's all just a memory from the past. That huge old cottonwood tree, that I thought was indestructible, died several years ago and now is rotting away on the ground. Therein lies a very important lesson of life that I will attempt to pass on to my wife, children,

Chapter 19 - REFLECTIONS

grandchildren, friends, and others that read this book.

Our life here on this earth is so uncertain. We plan for the future as if we will always be here, but just like that huge old tree, we will not last forever. As we grow older we realize this, and to some extent begin to accept it as a fact of life. What is hard for us to accept is that sometimes younger persons, who haven't lived a full life, are taken away unexpectedly. This is not meant to be depressing; far from it. Rather, it is to explain why we should savor each day by living life to the fullest while concentrating on those things that give our lives real meaning.

So what are those things in life that are of so much importance? Is it the wealth, possessions, and power that so many strive to achieve? Of course not, for all these things are taken away in an instant at our passing. It is natural for us to try to attempt to have good homes and to provide for our families needs, and we all like to have nice things. We just need to remember to keep everything in perspective. I could make a long list of all the things that I feel are of great importance in our lives. However, if we can just try to do our best to achieve the following there won't be any need of a long list, as this will pretty much cover everything.

This is what I believe we should do with and during our lives in the order of importance; God sent his son Jesus Christ here on earth to die for our sins in order that we might be saved and have everlasting life. All we have to do is believe, ask for forgiveness for our sins, and accept Jesus as our personal savior. Sounds so simple, yet many don't believe. Without this belief, we have no hope for the future, so this is of the utmost importance and must be the priority of our lives.

What did God tell us to do? Love God and love one another! This brings me to what I think is the second most important thing in our lives. If we love God and love one another, we will strive to do all we can to help others in any way we can. We must do this without any thought of rewards or praise. By doing this, we will build up a treasure worth more than all the wealth in the world, for no good work goes unnoticed by God. The Bible teaches us that salvation, freely given, does not mean that good works are unimportant. (Ephesians 2:10) God rewards us forever for our good works. (Matthew 16: 27) and (Revelation 22:12)

So if we truly believe and truly love, everything else pretty much falls into place. If we apply these two principles to all the decisions we make, we will be living our lives in the way I believe we should. Just imagine what the world would be like if everyone followed these two principles throughout their lives. (Maybe this is a glimpse of what heaven will be like.) Being human, we all sometimes fail to follow these two principles at times. So always remember this; When you stumble in your decisions as you go through life, get back up, put it behind you, and try to do better.

What we do today creates our memories of the past, lets try to make them all good ones.

T. R. T.

Lillian E (Thurman) Johnson

*Photograph Courtesy of
Herring Photographers taken in 1930
at age 23*

Chapter 20

Poems

By

Lillian E (Thurman) Johnson

L. E. J.

Here are two lost poems that I found that my Aunt Lillian E. (Thurman) Johnson who is now deceased, wrote in 1931.

Questing

You called me from the shadows,
Into the land of play;
My heart was filled with happiness;
Now you must go away.

You asked me for my answer,
To go or not to go.
To match mine to your eager steps,
Mine that are always slow.

You tell me of a world beyond,
Of lands and seas to roam.
How can I leave it all behind,
This place that's been my home?

And should I heed your trumpets call,
Would you be satisfied?
When years have passed, our journey done,
When strength and youth have died.

To find a haven of peace at last,
Away from the surging tide.
And grow to love the homely things,
With me close by your side?

L. E. J.

Parting

The end of the road and a parting,
The time has come for it all;
With sorrowful heart I linger,
And list to memories call.

The days and nights spent together,
Were full both of joy and of pain,
But oh! If time could repeat them,
I'd live them all over again.

A bright smile and a handclasp,
Best wishes throughout all the years.
But in my heart there's an aching,
And the shadow of slow falling tears.

L. E. J.

Chapter 21

Poems

By

Thomas R Thurman

T. R. T.

Here are several poems I have written over the years. This one I wrote when I got home from the hospital a few years ago from an operation for a ruptured appendix. It had ruptured on a Monday, and not realizing it, I didn't go to the doctor until Friday. They said if the poison had spread, I could have died. It is called:

Death Came Knocking

Death came knocking at my door,
To take me away forevermore.
I looked him in the eye and said,
I fear you not, I have no dread.

A power much greater than you are,
Is watching ore me from afar.
Some mission in life I must do,
The reason I have no fear of you.

Give me the reason, death said to me,
Forget the mission, I'll set you free.
I knew what he said was not true,
He wanted me not, that good thing to do.

To that power above, I looked up to Thee,
What mission in life, do you have for me?
Each day someone has a need,
So in that day, do a good deed.

T. R. T.

These next three poems are about friends and friendships. One of the purest relationships in this world, is that between "True Friends."

Your Friend

*Your friend always puts you first,
No matter what you do or say.
Whatever happens throughout the years,
It will always be that way.*

*Should the world turn against you,
Your friend will still be there.
To understand what went wrong,
Your friend will always care.*

*Should the miles separate us,
The friendship ever true.
For the heart knows no distance,
It's always there with you.*

*So my friend always remember,
Wherever you may be.
You'll never be alone again ,
Forever you and me.*

T. R. T.

The Trails in Our Lives

*(The trails we follow in our lives
determine who we are.)*

*Many trails to follow which one to take,
Our lives determined by the decisions we make.*

*Be careful to follow the trail that is right,
By making good choices, with good goals in sight.*

*As you follow this trail, be sure to learn,
To enjoy each day, it won't return.*

*If the way gets too high, too hard, or too steep,
Call on me, and this promise I'll keep.*

*To be there too help carry the load,
Till you reach an easier place in the road.*

*What do I want when this trail comes to an end?
Nothing I say, for you are my friend.*

T. R. T.

Footprints in the Sand

The wind swept across the land,
Erasing our footprints in the sand.
We had walked together for a while,
You had warmed my heart with your smile.

For our footprints I searched in vain,
Would we ever walk this way again?
Tears were flowing from my eyes,
I had never wanted us to say goodbyes.

Then in the sand I saw a faint track,
Side by side you had come back.
A friend like me you could never find,
Who cares so much and is so kind.

So when our footprints begin to stray,
Together we can always find a way.
No matter where we may be,
In the sand our footprints you and me.

T. R. T.

Mom always looked forward to the first robins that came each spring. So when she was in the nursing home dying of cancer in march of 2001 and I knew there was no hope for her to get any better, I saw the first robins of spring and wrote this poem for her.

He Sent the Robins

*Life is a mystery
or so they say,
Why did things
have to happen this way?*

*I've searched for the answer
everywhere it seems,
In my thoughts and prayers
and even my dreams.*

*Lord, send me a sign,
something to show,
To give hope to our lives
that we can know.*

*That life has real meaning
that there's hope for sure,
To give us strength
though we know there is no cure.*

*And now I know
everything will be ok,
For I saw the robins,
He sent them today.*

T. R. T.

When things seem hopeless believe and try and what you thought was impossible could come true.

The Little Butterfly

A little butterfly got caught in a sudden storm,
Its wings were oh so tattered and torn.
Others in the forest looked at her and said,
You'll never fly again before you're dead.

The little butterfly was very sad,
To fly again would make her glad.
A wise owl in the forest said,
Unfold your wings and raise your head.

It was a miracle her wings did grow,
Because she believed it made it so.
Suddenly she began to fly across the sky,
The most wonderful, beautiful, butterfly.

So when life's storms come to you,
And you feel there's something you cannot do.
Believe it will happen if you try,
And remember that beautiful little butterfly.

T. R. T.

These two poems are for my wife Connie, "The love of my life."

Those Eyes

Like yesterday I remember,
Those eyes that looked at me.
You had no way of knowing,
In them what I did see.

For you did not know me,
Or what I might do.
In those eyes I saw my future,
I knew it was with you.

More precious than diamonds,
They glowed in the night.
I had to win you over,
To my arms and hold you tight.

We've been together a long time now,
My wish, it had come true.
As I look into those eyes each day, I know,
I'll always be with you.

T. R. T.

I'll Love You More

As I look back through the years,
The days of laughter,
and the times of tears.
Why did I not realize what I had,
When times were good
and times were bad?

I should have known
from the very start,
That day when you first
gave me your heart.
If I could have known then
what I know now,
I'd go back and love you more,
if I knew how.

As sure as the earth
continues to turn,
Each day we grow older
we continue to learn.
The most important
thing in my life,
Was that day when
you became my wife.

This one thing
I know I'd do,
More love back
then I'd have for you,
We know not what
the future has in store,
I promise you this,
"I'll love you more."

T. R. T.

Unspoken Words

From the depths of our minds
there are words never spoken,
Inter most thought never shared,
For reasons unknown we never say them,
Hoping You'll know how much we cared.

Fear of misunderstanding seems to guide us,
As we continue in our silent way,
Are we bound to be this way forever?
Or will we find the courage some day?

To tell how much you mean to us,
As life swiftly passes by,
For all too soon it will be over,
And we'll be left wondering why.

And then as you kneel and say them,
In silence at the end of the day,
And you pray in some way they will hear you,
From under the ground where they lay.

So always remember,
This is the time you should share,
Those unspoken words you should say them,
To let them know how much you care.

T. R. T.

About the Author

*Thomas R Thurman on the summit of Mount Elbert
The highest mountain in the Rockies*

Thomas R. Thurman (Tom), the son of Ralph L. and Winifred L. Thurman was born on June 12, 1942 in Marion County Missouri, where he has lived on a farm all of his life. He has one sister, Beth Meyer, who lives in New Mexico with her husband, Mike. Tom met his wife, Connie, in the spring of 1968 and they were married on January 25, 1969. They have two children, a daughter, Cindi, and a son, Brad. Cindi and her husband, Paul Osborne, have three children, Brendon, Alex, and Trevor. Brad and his wife, Jacki also have three children, Keilynn, Thomas, and Carley. All of their grandchildren are active in sports and other activities, and Tom and Connie attend as many of them as possible. They are very proud and thankful for everyone in their family, and for all the fun times they have when they get together.

Tom and Connie are both active members in the Hunnewell United Methodist Church, where Tom serves as chairman of the board and teaches the adult Sunday school class during the spring quarter. Tom is now semi-retired from farming, and Connie is employed as the manager of the Monroe City Sheltered Workshop.

Tom has always had an adventurous spirit. In addition to the adventures covered in this book, he has also climbed two of Colorado's fourteeners (mountains with an elevation of fourteen thousand feet or higher), Windom Peak in the Weminuche Wilderness and Mount Elbert, which is the highest mountain in the Rockies. He also enjoys hiking, backpacking, running, skating, archery, hunting, fishing, canoeing, and driving his dune buggy. He keeps in shape during the winter months by running on a treadmill and lifting weights so he can keep doing all these different activities he enjoys.

Additional books may be purchased from the author by calling: (573) 439-5988 or E-mailing: tcthurman@marktwain.net.